Tall Ship Lace Filet Crochet Pattern

Tall Ship Lace Filet Crochet Pattern

Complete Instructions and Chart

designed by Carolyn Waite

edited by Claudia Botterweg

EIGHTTHREEPRESS
Phoenix, Arizona, USA

Original pattern design by Carolyn Waite, first published in 1927
Pattern rewritten, expanded, edited and charted by Claudia Botterweg,
published in 2015 by Eight Three Press
ISBN-13: 978-1507618745
ISBN-10: 1507618743
Every effort has been made to ensure that all the information in this book is accurate. If you have questions or
comments about this pattern, please contact Claudia Botterweg at
http://claudiabotterweg.com/contact

Contents

Introduction

Though originally intended for framing under glass as a serving tray, this effective design will be found equally pleasing when used as a panel or pillow cover, a chair back or as may be required. You can add an edging of your choice for a panel, chair back or pillow top, which will make the piece larger and add to its attractiveness.

Size & Yardage

The approximate size of the finished piece will change when made with different sizes of thread and hooks. Approximate yardage needed for each thread size varies also.

For best results, make a gauge swatch before you begin.

Size 5 thread (about 3.6 squares/inch)
Width: 28", Height: 25 ½"
Amount of thread required: 1,440 yards
Suggested hook: Size 3 steel

Size 10 thread (about 4.3 squares/inch)
Width: 23", Height: 20"
Amount of thread required: 912 yards
Suggested hook: Size 7 steel

Size 20 thread (about 4.5 squares/inch)
Width: 22", Height: 19"
Amount of thread required: 856 yards
Suggested hook: Size 10 steel

Size 30 thread (about 4.7 squares/inch)
Width: 21", Height: 18 ½"
Amount of thread required: 800 yards
Suggested hook: Size 11 steel

Size 50 thread (about 6 squares/inch)
  Width: 16", Height: 14 ½"
  Amount of thread required: 456 yards
  Suggested hook: Size 12 steel

Size 80 thread (about 7 squares/inch)
  Width: 14", Height: 12 ¾"
  Amount of thread required: 360 yards
  Suggested hook: Size 14 steel

Tall Ship Written Instructions

Abbreviations used in this pattern
( ) work instructions within parentheses as many times as directed
* * work instructions within asterisks as many times as directed
ch: chain stitch
dc: double crochet
sk: skip the indicated amount of stitches

Chain 245.
Row 1: Dc in 8th st from hook, (ch 2, sk 2, dc in next st) 79 times, turn. 80 squares.

Rows 2 to 7: Chain 5, dc in next dc, (ch 2, sk 2, dc in next st) 79 times, turn.

Row 8: Chain 5, dc in next dc, (ch 2, sk 2, dc in next st) 14 times, 12 dc, (ch 2, sk 2, dc in next st) 61 times, turn.

Row 9: Chain 5, dc in next dc, (ch 2, sk 2, dc in next st) 60 times, 15 dc, (ch 2, sk 2, dc in next st) 14 times, turn.

Row 10: Chain 5, dc in next dc, (ch 2, sk 2, dc in next st) 12 times, 6 dc, (ch 2, sk 2, dc in next st) 3 times, 6 dc, (ch 2, sk 2, dc in next st) 60 times, turn.

Row 11: Chain 5, dc in next dc, (ch 2, sk 2, dc in next st) 58 times, 9 dc, (ch 2, sk 2, dc in next st) 4 times, 6 dc, (ch 2, sk 2, dc in next st) 12 times, turn.

Row 12: Chain 5, dc in next dc, (ch 2, sk 2, dc in next st) 11 times, 3 dc, (ch 2, sk 2, dc in next st) 6 times, 6 dc, (ch 2, sk 2, dc in next st) 59 times, turn.

Row 13: Chain 5, dc in next dc, (ch 2, sk 2, dc in next st) 58 times, 3 dc, (ch 2, sk 2, dc in next st) 7 times, 3 dc, (ch 2, sk 2, dc in next st) 12 times, turn.

Row 14: Chain 5, dc in next dc, (ch 2, sk 2, dc in next st) 11 times, 6 dc, (ch 2, sk 2, dc in next st) 6 times, 3 dc, (ch 2, sk 2, dc in next st) 59 times, turn.

Row 15: Chain 5, dc in next dc, (ch 2, sk 2, dc in next st) 58 times, 3 dc, (ch 2, sk 2, dc in next st) 3 times, 3 dc, ch 2, sk 2, dc in next st, 6 dc, (ch 2, sk 2, dc in next st) 13 times, turn.

Row 16: Chain 5, dc in next dc, (ch 2, sk 2, dc in next st) 13 times, 6 dc, (ch 2, sk 2, dc in next st) 4 times, 3 dc, (ch 2, sk 2, dc in next st) 59 times, turn.

Row 17: Chain 5, dc in next dc, (ch 2, sk 2, dc in next st) 58 times, 3 dc, (ch 2, sk 2, dc in next st) 20 times, turn.

Row 18: Chain 5, dc in next dc, (ch 2, sk 2, dc in next st) 16 times, 6 dc, ch 2, sk 2, dc in next st, 3 dc, (ch 2, sk 2, dc in next st) 59 times, turn.

Row 19: Chain 5, dc in next dc, (ch 2, sk 2, dc in next st) 58 times, *3 dc, ch 2, sk 2, dc in next st* twice, 3 dc, (ch 2, sk 2, dc in next st) 16 times, turn.

Row 20: Chain 5, dc in next dc, (ch 2, sk 2, dc in next st) 18 times, 3 dc, (ch 2, sk 2, dc in next st) 60 times, turn.

Row 21: Chain 5, dc in next dc, (ch 2, sk 2, dc in next st) 28 times, 6 dc, (ch 2, sk 2, dc in next st) 29 times, 3 dc, (ch 2, sk 2, dc in next st) 19 times, turn.

Row 22: Chain 5, dc in next dc, (ch 2, sk 2, dc in next st) 19 times, 18 dc, (ch 2, sk 2, dc in next st) 17 times, 21 dc, (ch 2, sk 2, dc in next st) 30 times, turn.

Row 23: Chain 5, dc in next dc, (ch 2, sk 2, dc in next st) 30 times, 24 dc, (ch 2, sk 2, dc in next st) 14 times, 3 dc, (ch 2, sk 2, dc in next st) 5 times, 9 dc, (ch 2, sk 2, dc in next st) 18 times, turn.

Row 24: Chain 5, dc in next dc, (ch 2, sk 2, dc in next st) 7 times, 9 dc, (ch 2, sk 2, dc in next st) 6 times, 6 dc, (ch 2, sk 2, dc in next st) 7 times, 6 dc, (ch 2, sk 2, dc in next st) 10 times, 30 dc, (ch 2, sk 2, dc in next st) 32 times, turn.

Row 25: Chain 5, dc in next dc, (ch 2, sk 2, dc in next st) 32 times, 18 dc, (ch 2, sk 2, dc in next st) 13 times, 3 dc, (ch 2, sk 2, dc in next st) 9 times, 3 dc, (ch 2, sk 2, dc in next st) 5 times, 6 dc, ch 2, sk 2, dc in next st, 3 dc, (ch 2, sk 2, dc in next st) 8 times, turn.

Row 26: Chain 5, dc in next dc, (ch 2, sk 2, dc in next st) 6 times, 3 dc, (ch 2, sk 2, dc in next st) 3 times, 6 dc, (ch 2, sk 2, dc in next st) 4 times, 3 dc, (ch 2, sk 2, dc in next st) 9 times, 3 dc, (ch 2, sk 2, dc in next st) 8 times, 30 dc, (ch 2, sk 2, dc in next st) 34 times, turn.

Row 27: Chain 5, dc in next dc, (ch 2, sk 2, dc in next st) 27 times, 3 dc, (ch 2, sk 2, dc in next st) 6 times, 21 dc, (ch 2, sk 2, dc in next st) 3 times, 9 dc, (ch 2, sk 2, dc in next st) 4 times, 3 dc, (ch 2, sk 2, dc in next st) 9 times, 3 dc, *(ch 2, sk 2, dc in next st) 4 times, 3 dc* twice, (ch 2, sk 2, dc in next st) 7 times, turn.

Row 28: Chain 5, dc in next dc, (ch 2, sk 2, dc in next st) 6 times, 3 dc, (ch 2, sk 2, dc in next st) 4 times, 3 dc, (ch 2, sk 2, dc in next st) 3 times, 3 dc, (ch 2, sk 2, dc in next st) 9 times, 3 dc, (ch 2, sk 2, dc in next st) 6 times, 33 dc, (ch 2, sk 2, dc in next st) 7 times, 3 dc, (ch 2, sk 2, dc in next st) 28 times, turn.

Row 29: Chain 5, dc in next dc, (ch 2, sk 2, dc in next st) 27 times, 6 dc, (ch 2, sk 2, dc in next st) 7 times, 27 dc, ch 2, sk 2, dc in next st, 9 dc, (ch 2, sk 2, dc in next st) 13 times, *3 dc, (ch 2, sk 2, dc in next st) 3 times* twice, 3 dc, (ch 2, sk 2, dc in next st) 8 times, turn.

Row 30: Chain 5, dc in next dc, (ch 2, sk 2, dc in next st) 11 times, *3 dc, (ch 2, sk 2, dc in next st) 3 times* twice, 6 dc, (ch 2, sk 2, dc in next st) 5 times, 12 dc, ch 2, sk 2, dc in next st, 3 dc, ch 2, sk 2, dc in next st, 24 dc, (ch 2, sk 2, dc in next st) 7 times, 9 dc, (ch 2, sk 2, dc in next st) 28 times, turn.

Row 31: Chain 5, dc in next dc, (ch 2, sk 2, dc in next st) 27 times, 12 dc, (ch 2, sk 2, dc in next st) 7 times, 18 dc, (ch 2, sk 2, dc in next st) 2 times, 9 dc, ch 2, sk 2, dc in next st,12 dc, (ch 2, sk 2, dc in next st) 2 times, 6 dc, ch 2, sk 2, dc in next st, 3 dc, (ch 2, sk

2, dc in next st) 2 times, 9 dc, ch 2, sk 2, dc in next st, 3 dc, (ch 2, sk 2, dc in next st) 12 times, turn.

Row 32: Chain 5, dc in next dc, (ch 2, sk 2, dc in next st) 11 times, 3 dc, ch 2, sk 2, dc in next st, 6 dc, ch 2, sk 2, dc in next st, 3 dc, (ch 2, sk 2, dc in next st) 4 times, 3 dc, ch 2, sk 2, dc in next st, 21 dc, ch 2, sk 2, dc in next st, 3 dc, (ch 2, sk 2, dc in next st) 2 times, 15 dc, (ch 2, sk 2, dc in next st) 7 times, 12 dc, (ch 2, sk 2, dc in next st) 29 times, turn.

Row 33: Chain 5, dc in next dc, (ch 2, sk 2, dc in next st) 28 times, 15 dc, (ch 2, sk 2, dc in next st) 7 times, 12 dc, (ch 2, sk 2, dc in next st) 2 times, 12 dc, ch 2, sk 2, dc in next st, 12 dc, (ch 2, sk 2, dc in next st) 2 times, 3 dc, (ch 2, sk 2, dc in next st) 3 times, 3 dc, (ch 2, sk 2, dc in next st) 2 times, 3 dc, ch 2, sk 2, dc in next st, 3 dc, (ch 2, sk 2, dc in next st) 12 times, turn.

Row 34: Chain 5, dc in next dc, (ch 2, sk 2, dc in next st) 11 times, 3 dc, ch 2, sk 2, dc in next st, 3 dc, (ch 2, sk 2, dc in next st) 3 times, 3 dc, ch 2, sk 2, dc in next st, 6 dc, ch 2, sk 2, dc in next st, 21 dc, ch 2, sk 2, dc in next st, 3 dc, (ch 2, sk 2, dc in next st) 3 times, 9 dc, (ch 2, sk 2, dc in next st) 7 times, 18 dc, (ch 2, sk 2, dc in next st) 29 times, turn.

Row 35: Chain 5, dc in next dc, (ch 2, sk 2, dc in next st) 28 times, 21 dc, (ch 2, sk 2, dc in next st) 7 times, 6 dc, (ch 2, sk 2, dc in next st) 3 times, *12 dc, ch 2, sk 2, dc in next st* twice, 6 dc, *ch 2, sk 2, dc in next st, 3 dc* 4 times, (ch 2, sk 2, dc in next st) 12 times, turn.

Row 36: Chain 5, dc in next dc, (ch 2, sk 2, dc in next st) 13 times, 3 dc, ch 2, sk 2, dc in next st, 9 dc, ch 2, sk 2, dc in next st, 3 dc, (ch 2, sk 2, dc in next st) 2 times, 18 dc, ch 2, sk 2, dc in next st, 6 dc, (ch 2, sk 2, dc in next st) 3 times, 3 dc, (ch 2, sk 2, dc in next st) 6 times, 27 dc, (ch 2, sk 2, dc in next st) 29 times, turn.

Row 37: Chain 5, dc in next dc, (ch 2, sk 2, dc in next st) 29 times, 6 dc, ch 2, sk 2, dc in next st, 24 dc, (ch 2, sk 2, dc in next st) 4 times, 3 dc, (ch 2, sk 2, dc in next st) 2 times, 30 dc, ch 2, sk 2, dc in next st, 3 dc, *(ch 2, sk 2, dc in next st) 2 times, 3 dc* twice, (ch 2, sk 2, dc in next st) 14 times, turn.

Row 38: Chain 5, dc in next dc, (ch 2, sk 2, dc in next st) 8 times, 9 dc, (ch 2, sk 2, dc in next st) 2 times, 3 dc, (ch 2, sk 2, dc in next st) 5 times, 3 dc, ch 2, sk 2, dc in next st, 27 dc, (ch 2, sk 2, dc in next st) 5 times, 24 dc, (ch 2, sk 2, dc in next st) 3 times, 6 dc, (ch 2, sk 2, dc in next st) 31 times, turn.

Row 39: Chain 5, dc in next dc, (ch 2, sk 2, dc in next st) 30 times, 51 dc, ch 2, sk 2, dc in next st, 27 dc, ch 2, sk 2, dc in next st, 6 dc, (ch 2, sk 2, dc in next st) 4 times, 3 dc, ch 2, sk 2, dc in next st, 3 dc, (ch 2, sk 2, dc in next st) 3 times, 6 dc, (ch 2, sk 2, dc in next st) 7 times, turn.

Row 40: Chain 5, dc in next dc, (ch 2, sk 2, dc in next st) 6 times, 3 dc, (ch 2, sk 2, dc in next st) 4 times, 3 dc, ch 2, sk 2, dc in next st, 3 dc, (ch 2, sk 2, dc in next st) 6 times, 21 dc, ch 2, sk 2, dc in next st, 6 dc, (ch 2, sk 2, dc in next st) 2 times, 48 dc, ch 2, sk 2, dc in next st, 9 dc, (ch 2, sk 2, dc in next st) 11 times, 6 dc, (ch 2, sk 2, dc in next st) 14 times, turn.

Row 41: Chain 5, dc in next dc, (ch 2, sk 2, dc in next st) 13 times, 9 dc, (ch 2, sk 2, dc in next st) 6 times, 21 dc, ch 2, sk 2, dc in next st, 6 dc, (ch 2, sk 2, dc in next st) 2 times, 33 dc, (ch 2, sk 2, dc in next st) 3 times, 33 dc, ch 2, sk 2, dc in next st, 3 dc, (ch 2, sk 2, dc in next st) 3 times, 3 dc, ch 2, sk 2, dc in next st, 3 dc, *(ch 2, sk 2, dc in next st) 2 times, 3 dc* twice, (ch 2, sk 2, dc in next st) 6 times, turn.

Row 42: Chain 5, dc in next dc, (ch 2, sk 2, dc in next st) 5 times, 3 dc, (ch 2, sk 2, dc in next st) 3 times, *3 dc, ch 2, sk 2, dc in next st* twice, *3 dc, (ch 2, sk 2, dc in next st) 2 times* twice, 24 dc, ch 2, sk 2, dc in next st, 3 dc, (ch 2, sk 2, dc in next st) 4 times, 24 dc, (ch 2, sk 2, dc in next st) 3 times, 9 dc, (ch 2, sk 2, dc in next st) 2 times, 45 dc, (ch 2, sk 2, dc in next st) 15 times, turn.

Row 43: Chain 5, dc in next dc, (ch 2, sk 2, dc in next st) 15 times, 42 dc, (ch 2, sk 2, dc in next st) 2 times, 18 dc, (ch 2, sk 2, dc in next st) 4 times, 9 dc, (ch 2, sk 2, dc in next st) 5 times, 33 dc, ch 2, sk 2, dc in next st, 9 dc, (ch 2, sk 2, dc in next st) 2 times, 3 dc, ch 2, sk 2, dc in next st, 6 dc, ch 2, sk 2, dc in next st, 3 dc, (ch 2, sk 2, dc in next st) 7 times, turn.

Row 44: Chain 5, dc in next dc, (ch 2, sk 2, dc in next st) 7 times, 6 dc, (ch 2, sk 2, dc in next st) 3 times, *3 dc, (ch 2, sk 2, dc in next st) 2 times* twice, 27 dc, (ch 2, sk 2, dc in next st) 8 times, 33 dc, (ch 2, sk 2, dc in next st) 2 times, 45 dc, (ch 2, sk 2, dc in next st) 16 times, turn.

Row 45: Chain 5, dc in next dc, (ch 2, sk 2, dc in next st) 16 times, 24 dc, (ch 2, sk 2, dc in next st) 3 times, 9 dc, (ch 2, sk 2, dc in next st) 2 times, 33 dc, (ch 2, sk 2, dc in next st) 8 times, 27 dc, *(ch 2, sk 2, dc in next st) 2 times, 3 dc* twice, (ch 2, sk 2, dc in next st) 13 times, turn.

Row 46: Chain 5, dc in next dc, (ch 2, sk 2, dc in next st) 12 times, *3 dc, (ch 2, sk 2, dc in next st) 2 times* twice, 27 dc, (ch 2, sk 2, dc in next st) 4 times, 9 dc, (ch 2, sk 2, dc in next st) 2 times, 30 dc, ch 2, sk 2, dc in next st, 6 dc, (ch 2, sk 2, dc in next st) 2 times, 6 dc, ch 2, sk 2, dc in next st, 24 dc, (ch 2, sk 2, dc in next st) 17 times, turn.

Row 47: Chain 5, dc in next dc, (ch 2, sk 2, dc in next st) 17 times, 24 dc, ch 2, sk 2, dc in next st, 12 dc, (ch 2, sk 2, dc in next st) 2 times, 21 dc, (ch 2, sk 2, dc in next st) 3 times, 12 dc, (ch 2, sk 2, dc in next st) 5 times, 27 dc, *(ch 2, sk 2, dc in next st) 2 times, 3 dc* twice, (ch 2, sk 2, dc in next st) 13 times, turn.

Row 48: Chain 5, dc in next dc, (ch 2, sk 2, dc in next st) 12 times, *3 dc, (ch 2, sk 2, dc in next st) 2 times* twice, 33 dc, (ch 2, sk 2, dc in next st) 3 times, 21 dc, (ch 2, sk 2, dc in next st) 8 times, 15 dc, ch 2, sk 2, dc in next st, 12 dc, (ch 2, sk 2, dc in next st) 2 times, 6 dc, (ch 2, sk 2, dc in next st) 18 times, turn.

Row 49: Chain 5, dc in next dc, (ch 2, sk 2, dc in next st) 18 times, 9 dc, (ch 2, sk 2, dc in next st) 3 times, 6 dc, ch 2, sk 2, dc in next st, 54 dc, (ch 2, sk 2, dc in next st) 2 times, 39 dc, (ch 2, sk 2, dc in next st) 2 times, 3 dc, (ch 2, sk 2, dc in next st) 16 times, turn.

Row 50: Chain 5, dc in next dc, (ch 2, sk 2, dc in next st) 11 times, 3 dc, (ch 2, sk 2, dc in next st) 3 times, *3 dc, (ch 2, sk 2, dc in next st) 2 times* twice, 18 dc, *ch 2, sk 2, dc in next st, 3 dc* twice, (ch 2, sk 2, dc in next st) 2 times, 54 dc, ch 2, sk 2, dc in next st, 24 dc, (ch 2, sk 2, dc in next st) 19 times, turn.

Row 51: Chain 5, dc in next dc, (ch 2, sk 2, dc in next st) 19 times, 24 dc, ch 2, sk 2, dc in next st, 18 dc, (ch 2, sk 2, dc in next st) 2 times, 3 dc, ch 2, sk 2, dc in next st, 18 dc, (ch 2, sk 2, dc in next st) 3 times, 30 dc, ch 2, sk 2, dc in next st, 3 dc, (ch 2, sk 2, dc in next st) 2 times, 6 dc, (ch 2, sk 2, dc in next st) 3 times, 3 dc, (ch 2, sk 2, dc in next st) 12 times, turn.

Row 52: Chain 5, dc in next dc, (ch 2, sk 2, dc in next st) 11 times, 3 dc, (ch 2, sk 2, dc in next st) 3 times, 15 dc, ch 2, sk 2, dc in next st, 18 dc, *ch 2, sk 2, dc in next st, 3 dc* twice, (ch 2, sk 2, dc in next st) 3 times, 15 dc, (ch 2, sk 2, dc in next st) 4 times, 18 dc, (ch 2, sk 2, dc in next st) 2 times, 3 dc, (ch 2, sk 2, dc in next st) 4 times, 9 dc, (ch 2, sk 2, dc in next st) 7 times, 6 dc, (ch 2, sk 2, dc in next st) 11 times, turn.

Row 53: Chain 5, dc in next dc, (ch 2, sk 2, dc in next st) 11 times, 6 dc, (ch 2, sk 2, dc in next st) 7 times, 24 dc, ch 2, sk 2, dc in next st, 21 dc, (ch 2, sk 2, dc in next st) 4 times, 12 dc, (ch 2, sk 2, dc in next st) 3 times, 33 dc, (ch 2, sk 2, dc in next st) 2 times, 6 dc, (ch 2, sk 2, dc in next st) 4 times, 3 dc, (ch 2, sk 2, dc in next st) 12 times, turn.

Row 54: Row (ch 2, sk 2, dc in next st) 11 times, 3 dc, (ch 2, sk 2, dc in next st) 6 times, 27 dc, *ch 2, sk 2, dc in next st, 3 dc* twice, (ch 2, sk 2, dc in next st) 2 times, 6 dc, (ch 2, sk 2, dc in next st) 11 times, 6 dc, ch 2, sk 2, dc in next st, 24 dc, (ch 2, sk 2, dc in next st) 7 times, 6 dc, (ch 2, sk 2, dc in next st) 13 times, turn.

Row 55: Chain 5, dc in next dc, (ch 2, sk 2, dc in next st) 12 times, 9 dc, (ch 2, sk 2, dc in next st) 6 times, 27 dc, ch 2, sk 2, dc in next st, 6 dc, (ch 2, sk 2, dc in next st) 5 times, 15 dc, ch 2, sk 2, dc in next st, 3 dc, (ch 2, sk 2, dc in next st) 2 times, 39 dc, (ch 2, sk 2, dc in next st) 2 times, 3 dc, (ch 2, sk 2, dc in next st) 3 times, 3 dc, (ch 2, sk 2, dc in next st) 12 times, turn.

Row 56: Chain 5, dc in next dc, (ch 2, sk 2, dc in next st) 11 times, 3 dc, (ch 2, sk 2, dc in next st) 3 times, 3 dc, (ch 2, sk 2, dc in next st) 2 times, 27 dc, *ch 2, sk 2, dc in next st, 3 dc* twice, (ch 2, sk 2, dc in next st) 4 times, 15 dc, (ch 2, sk 2, dc in next st) 4 times, 9 dc, ch 2, sk 2, dc in next st, 24 dc, (ch 2, sk 2, dc in next st) 7 times, 6 dc, (ch 2, sk 2, dc in next st) 14·times, turn.

Row 57: Chain 5, dc in next dc, (ch 2, sk 2, dc in next st) 13 times, 6 dc, (ch 2, sk 2, dc in next st) 17 times, *15 dc, ch 2, sk 2, dc in next st* twice, 6 dc, ch 2, sk 2, dc in next st, 39 dc, (ch 2, sk 2, dc in next st) 2 times, 3 dc, (ch 2, sk 2, dc in next st) 3 times, 3 dc, (ch 2, sk 2, dc in next st) 12 times, turn.

Row 58: Chain 5, dc in next dc, (ch 2, sk 2, dc in next st) 11 times, 3 dc, (ch 2, sk 2, dc in next st) 3 times, 3 dc, (ch 2, sk 2, dc in next st) 2 times, 27 dc, (ch 2, sk 2, dc in next st) 4 times, 24 dc, (ch 2, sk 2, dc in next st) 2 times, 15 dc, (ch 2, sk 2, dc in next st) 17 times, 3 dc, (ch 2, sk 2, dc in next st) 15 times, turn.

Row 59: Chain 5, dc in next dc, (ch 2, sk 2, dc in next st) 14 times, 6 dc, (ch 2, sk 2, dc in next st) 17 times, 15 dc, ch 2, sk 2, dc in next st, 33 dc, ch 2, sk 2, dc in next st, 21 dc, (ch 2, sk 2, dc in next st) 4 times, 3 dc, (ch 2, sk 2, dc in next st) 3 times, 3 dc, (ch 2, sk 2, dc in next st) 12 times, turn.

Row 60: Chain 5, dc in next dc, (ch 2, sk 2, dc in next st) 11 times, 3 dc, (ch 2, sk 2, dc in next st) 3 times, 3 dc, (ch 2, sk 2, dc in next st) 5 times, 18 dc, (ch 2, sk 2, dc in next st) 2 times, 30 dc, ch 2, sk 2, dc in next st, 15 dc, (ch 2, sk 2, dc in next st) 16 times, 6 dc, (ch 2, sk 2, dc in next st) 16 times, turn.

Row 61: Chain 5, dc in next dc, (ch 2, sk 2, dc in next st) 25 times, 3 dc, (ch 2, sk 2, dc in next st) 8 times, 15 dc, ch 2, sk 2, dc in next st, 6 dc, ch 2, sk 2, dc in next st, 18 dc, (ch 2, sk 2, dc in next st) 2 times, 15 dc, (ch 2, sk 2, dc in next st) 6 times, 3 dc, (ch 2, sk 2, dc in next st) 3 times, 3 dc, (ch 2, sk 2, dc in next st) 12 times, turn.

Row 62: Chain 5, dc in next dc, (ch 2, sk 2, dc in next st) 11 times, 3 dc, (ch 2, sk 2, dc in next st) 3 times, 3 dc, (ch 2, sk 2, dc in next st) 2 times, 6 dc, (ch 2, sk 2, dc in next st) 4 times, 6 dc, (ch 2, sk 2, dc in next st) 3 times, 6 dc, (ch 2, sk 2, dc in next st) 4 times, 9 dc, ch 2, sk 2, dc in next st, 15 dc, (ch 2, sk 2, dc in next st) 6 times, 9 dc, (ch 2, sk 2, dc in next st) 26 times, turn.

Row 63: Chain 5, dc in next dc, (ch 2, sk 2, dc in next st) 26 times, 9 dc, (ch 2, sk 2, dc in next st) 6 times, 15 dc, ch 2, sk 2, dc in next st, 24 dc, (ch 2, sk 2, dc in next st) 3 times, 6 dc, (ch 2, sk 2, dc in next st) 3 times, 12 dc, ch 2, sk 2, dc in next st, 3 dc, (ch 2, sk 2, dc in next st) 3 times, 3 dc, (ch 2, sk 2, dc in next st) 12 times, turn.

Row 64: Chain 5, dc in next dc, (ch 2, sk 2, dc in next st) 11 times, 3 dc, (ch 2, sk 2, dc in next st) 3 times, 3 dc, ch 2, sk 2, dc in next st, 3 dc, (ch 2, sk 2, dc in next st) 2 times, 6 dc, (ch 2, sk 2, dc in next st) 4 times, 3 dc, (ch 2, sk 2, dc in next st) 3 times, 21 dc, (ch 2, sk 2, dc in next st) 11 times, 6 dc, (ch 2, sk 2, dc in next st) 29 times, turn.

Row 65: Chain 5, dc in next dc, (ch 2, sk 2, dc in next st) 28 times, 6 dc, (ch 2, sk 2, dc in next st) 12 times, 18 dc, (ch 2, sk 2, dc in next st) 2 times, 3 dc, *(ch 2, sk 2, dc in next st) 5 times, 3 dc* twice, (ch 2, sk 2, dc in next st) 3 times, 3 dc, (ch 2, sk 2, dc in next st) 12 times, turn.

Row 66: Chain 5, dc in next dc, (ch 2, sk 2, dc in next st) 11 times, 3 dc, *(ch 2, sk 2, dc in next st) 3 times, 6 dc* twice, (ch 2, sk 2, dc in next st) 7 times, 6 dc, (ch 2, sk 2, dc in next st) 2 times, 9 dc, (ch 2, sk 2, dc in next st) 11 times, 6 dc, (ch 2, sk 2, dc in next st) 30 times, turn.

Row 67: Chain 5, dc in next dc, (ch 2, sk 2, dc in next st) 30 times, 3 dc, (ch 2, sk 2, dc in next st) 12 times, 18 dc, (ch 2, sk 2, dc in next st) 8 times, 15 dc, (ch 2, sk 2, dc in next st) 3 times, 6 dc, (ch 2, sk 2, dc in next st) 12 times, turn.

Row 68: Chain 5, dc in next dc, (ch 2, sk 2, dc in next st) 11 times, 6 dc, (ch 2, sk 2, dc in next st) 4 times, 9 dc, (ch 2, sk 2, dc in next st) 8 times, 21 dc, (ch 2, sk 2, dc in next st) 44 times, turn.

Row 69: Chain 5, dc in next dc, (ch 2, sk 2, dc in next st) 44 times, 21 dc, (ch 2, sk 2, dc in next st) 2 times, 3 dc, (ch 2, sk 2, dc in next st) 9 times, 9 dc, (ch 2, sk 2, dc in next st) 13 times, turn.

Row 70: Chain 5, dc in next dc, (ch 2, sk 2, dc in next st) 11 times, 6 dc, (ch 2, sk 2, dc in next st) 2 times, 3 dc, (ch 2, sk 2, dc in next st) 9 times, 27 dc, (ch 2, sk 2, dc in next st) 45 times, turn.

Row 71: Chain 5, dc in next dc, (ch 2, sk 2, dc in next st) 44 times, 27 dc, (ch 2, sk 2, dc in next st) 7 times, 6 dc, (ch 2, sk 2, dc in next st) 4 times, 3 dc, ch 2, sk 2, dc in next st, 3 dc, (ch 2, sk 2, dc in next st) 10 times, turn.

Row 72: Chain 5, dc in next dc, (ch 2, sk 2, dc in next st) 10 times, 6 dc, (ch 2, sk 2, dc in next st) 5 times, 6 dc, (ch 2, sk 2, dc in next st) 7 times, 21 dc, (ch 2, sk 2, dc in next st) 19 times, 3 dc, (ch 2, sk 2, dc in next st) 26 times, turn.

Row 73: Chain 5, dc in next dc, (ch 2, sk 2, dc in next st) 26 times, 3 dc, (ch 2, sk 2, dc in next st) 18 times, 18 dc, (ch 2, sk 2, dc in next st) 8 times, 3 dc, (ch 2, sk 2, dc in next st) 19 times, turn.

Row 74: Chain 5, dc in next dc, (ch 2, sk 2, dc in next st) 19 times, 3 dc, (ch 2, sk 2, dc in next st) 8 times, 15 dc, (ch 2, sk 2, dc in next st) 17 times, 3 dc, (ch 2, sk 2, dc in next st) 28 times, turn.

Row 75: Chain 5, dc in next dc, (ch 2, sk 2, dc in next st) 28 times, 6 dc, (ch 2, sk 2, dc in next st) 9 times, 3 dc, (ch 2, sk 2, dc in next st) 17 times, 6 dc, (ch 2, sk 2, dc in next st) 20 times, turn.

Row 76: Chain 5, dc in next dc, (ch 2, sk 2, dc in next st) 20 times, 3 dc, (ch 2, sk 2, dc in next st) 15 times, 9 dc, (ch 2, sk 2, dc in next st) 10 times, 3 dc, (ch 2, sk 2, dc in next st) 29 times, turn.

Row 77: Chain 5, dc in next dc, (ch 2, sk 2, dc in next st) 27 times, 6 dc, (ch 2, sk 2, dc in next st) 11 times, 12 dc, (ch 2, sk 2, dc in next st) 12 times, 6 dc, (ch 2, sk 2, dc in next st) 21 times, turn.

Row 78: Chain 5, dc in next dc, (ch 2, sk 2, dc in next st) 21 times, 3 dc, (ch 2, sk 2, dc in next st) 12 times, 3 dc, (ch 2, sk 2, dc in next st) 15 times, 3 dc, (ch 2, sk 2, dc in next st) 28 times, turn.

Row 79: Chain 5, dc in next dc, (ch 2, sk 2, dc in next st) 27 times, 3 dc, (ch 2, sk 2, dc in next st) 15 times, 6 dc, (ch 2, sk 2, dc in next st) 11 times, 3 dc, (ch 2, sk 2, dc in next st) 22 times, turn.

Row 80: Chain 5, dc in next dc, (ch 2, sk 2, dc in next st) 21 times, 3 dc, (ch 2, sk 2, dc in next st) 10 times, 3 dc, (ch 2, sk 2, dc in next st) 46 times, turn.

Row 81: Chain 5, dc in next dc, (ch 2, sk 2, dc in next st) 56 times, 3 dc, (ch 2, sk 2, dc in next st) 22 times, turn.

Row 82: Chain 5, dc in next dc, (ch 2, sk 2, dc in next st) 16 times, 6 dc, (ch 2, sk 2, dc in next st) 3 times, 3 dc, (ch 2, sk 2, dc in next st) 57 times, turn.

Row 83: Chain 5, dc in next dc, (ch 2, sk 2, dc in next st) 56 times, 3 dc, (ch 2, sk 2, dc in next st) 2 times, 6 dc, ch 2, sk 2, dc in next st, 3 dc, (ch 2, sk 2, dc in next st) 16 times, turn.

Row 84: Chain 5, dc in next dc, (ch 2, sk 2, dc in next st) 14 times, 6 dc, (ch 2, sk 2, dc in next st) 2 times, 3 dc, ch 2, sk 2, dc in next st, 6 dc, (ch 2, sk 2, dc in next st) 14 times, 3 dc, (ch 2, sk 2, dc in next st) 42 times, turn.

Row 85: Chain 5, dc in next dc, (ch 2, sk 2, dc in next st) 42 times, 6 dc, (ch 2, sk 2, dc in next st) 2 times, 3 dc, (ch 2, sk 2, dc in next st) 10 times, 9 dc, (ch 2, sk 2, dc in next st) 2 times, 6 dc, (ch 2, sk 2, dc in next st) 15 times, turn.

Row 86: Chain 5, dc in next dc, (ch 2, sk 2, dc in next st) 15 times, 3 dc, (ch 2, sk 2, dc in next st) 3 times, 6 dc, (ch 2, sk 2, dc in next st) 11 times, 6 dc, (ch 2, sk 2, dc in next st) 45 times, turn.

Row 87: Chain 5, dc in next dc, (ch 2, sk 2, dc in next st) 45 times, 3 dc, (ch 2, sk 2, dc in next st) 12 times, 12 dc, (ch 2, sk 2, dc in next st) 17 times, turn.

Row 88: Chain 5, dc in next dc, (ch 2, sk 2, dc in next st) 17 times, 6 dc, (ch 2, sk 2, dc in next st) 13 times, 3 dc, (ch 2, sk 2, dc in next st) 46 times, turn.

Row 89: Chain 5, dc in next dc, (ch 2, sk 2, dc in next st) 45 times, 3 dc, (ch 2, sk 2, dc in next st) 33 times, turn.

Row 90: Chain 5, dc in next dc, (ch 2, sk 2, dc in next st) 31 times, 3 dc, (ch 2, sk 2, dc in next st) 47 times, turn.

Row 91: Chain 5, dc in next dc, (ch 2, sk 2, dc in next st) 46 times, 3 dc, (ch 2, sk 2, dc in next st) 32 times, turn.

Row 92: Chain 5, dc in next dc, (ch 2, sk 2, dc in next st) 30 times, 3 dc, (ch 2, sk 2, dc in next st) 48 times, turn.

Rows 93 to 100: Chain 5, dc in next dc, (ch 2, sk 2, dc in next st) 79 times, turn.

This completes the lace.

Tall Ship Chart

Chain 245.
Work odd rows left to right. Work even rows right to left.
Chain 5 for the first space in each row.

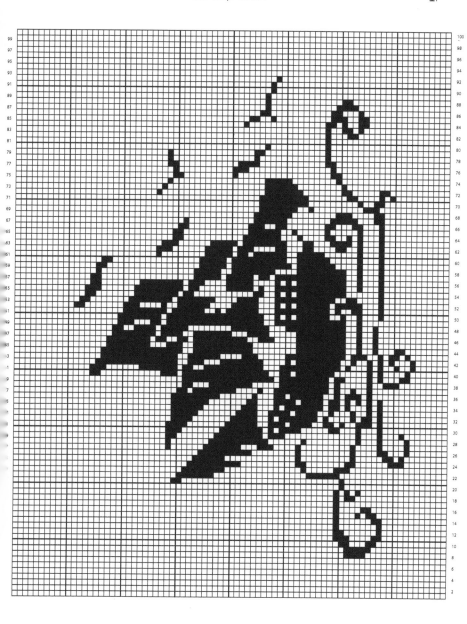

Finishing

Rigging

If preferred, the rigging may be omitted on articles such as pillow tops.

A rather unusual feature, which makes the design more realistic, is the addition of mast-tops from which the pennants fly, stays and other "nautical rigging," for which lines of thread serve.

If to be used for a tray the work should be carefully pressed and mounted upon a piece of cardboard, smoothly covered with fast-color linen or other suitable material of any desired tint—light green was used in this instance. The card should be about an inch larger all around than the lace, or have a margin which will be just covered by the frame, and the lace is mounted evenly upon it; then the lines of thread may be caught through the card and firmly held.

The thread is used double and each line repeated, so that the "stays" are four-stranded; and where these are long they are caught down by tiny stitches taken across at intervals. For example, counting 26 spaces on the 17th row bring your needle up through the top of next dc, pass over next 3 rows diagonally, put the needle down at base of 1st of 6 dc of 21st row, repeat once to give the four strands, bring the needle up in the 29th space of 19th row, pass diagonally across the line to the right, go down through the 33rd of the 60 spaces of the 20th row, repeat, coming up and going down in the same place always, come up through the next space at left, or 32nd space, carry the stay to the next sail, as shown, and continue; the lines are all put in in the same manner.

Finishing

Then when the piece is completed, it is framed and ready for service.

If to be used for other purposes, press and mount the lace on cardboard by means of thumb-tacks; then fasten the lines of thread, where needed, by small, firm buttonhole-stitches or knots taken around or into a double crochet, as required. A little variation in the lines is not material, but they should not be pulled too tightly, so that the lace will not be drawn or puckered. The mounting will prevent this, and the tacks are readily removed when the work is finished.

Hints & Tips

Wash your hands before you pick up your project to work on. Keeping your hands clean while you work will help to avoid stains on your piece of lace.

When you're finished, weave in ends of thread by pulling the thread through several stitches with your hook.

To block your lace, dampen it and use a warm iron to block it in to shape. I like to use a little bit of spray starch to finish it off.

Filet crochet patterns are made up of two elements. The first is the space, which is made up of a double crochet, chain two, skip two stitches, and double crochet in the next stitch. The second is the block, which is made of a double crochet, double crochet in the next two stitches, and double crochet in the next stitch.

When you make a block over a space from the previous row, just double crochet into the space. Don't worry about crocheting into each chain.

You can follow a chart instead of a written pattern (a chart is included with this pattern). When you use the chart, you just need to remember that the beginning of each row starts with either chain three (for a block) or chain five (for a space). You can also use the chart to check your progress if you're using the written instructions.

Filet crochet blocks and spaces are not quite square, so your finished project won't look as squared off as the chart.

Visit http://claudiabotterweg.com/crochet for tips, hints and more about lace crochet.

I hope you enjoyed making this beautiful piece of lace. Tell your friends where you got the pattern.

About the Editor

Claudia Botterweg learned how to crochet in third grade, and by the time she left home for college she had completed 8 rows on a ripple afghan. At Ohio State, she found herself living across the street from a vintage clothing store, and spent most of her budget on vintage clothes. She began repairing clothes in exchange for store credit. One of her tasks was to make camisoles with vintage crocheted lace yokes.

After college, Claudia inherited a tin full of several used balls of tatting thread, a tatting shuttle, and a size 14 steel crochet hook from her grandmother. She made some lace edgings from an old crochet pattern book, became fascinated with lace, and graduated to making doilies. In the 1980s, she made hundreds of lace collars and sold them at craft fairs. She also designed her own camisole yokes and made camisoles to sell.

Recently, Claudia acquired a stack of vintage patterns. She has been busily translating the patterns from vintage instructions, making them easy for beginning and intermediate crocheters to read. She is writing instructions when only charts were provided, and making charts when only written instructions were provided.

Claudia hopes that a new generation of crocheters will learn how to make beautiful lace to decorate themselves, their friends and families, and their homes.

http://ClaudiaBotterweg.com

More Patterns from Claudia Botterweg

Grape & Leaf Altar Lace
Ivy Lace Scarf End
Beverly Lace & Insertion
Dogwood Blossom Lace Curtain
Two Peacocks Lace Curtain
Quilt Block Lace Edging & Insertion
Two Dragons Lace Curtain
Lyre Lace Scarf End
Butterfly Lace Camisole Yoke
Daffodil Lace Curtain
Rose Lace & Insertion
Daffodil Altar Lace
Garden Trellis Lace Centerpiece
Elegant Dragons Lace Curtain
Regal Peacocks Lace Curtain
Morning Glory Lace & Insertion
Nottingham Apple Lace Luncheon Set Filet Crochet Pattern
Lion Lace Panel Filet Crochet Pattern
Butterfly Lace Table Runner Filet Crochet Pattern
Crochet Journal
Knitting Journal
Quilting Journal
Rose Insertion Filet Crochet Pattern
Diamonds Insertion & Edging Filet Crochet Pattern

Printed in Great Britain
by Amazon

Lifelines

Alex Johnston
with Jonathon Porritt

Illustrated by McLachlan

Introduction by Jonathon Porritt
Foreword by Friends of the Earth

RED FOX

To my Dad, Mum and Georgia.

Acknowledgement

I would like to say a very big thank you to *all* those people who wrote to me. And particularly to those whose letters could not be included in the text because there just wasn't room. Grahame Dangerfield, Philip Allen, Lou Ellis, *and* my sister, Marina are just a few of those people. They all went to a lot of trouble to write, and I wish there had been room to include ALL the letters I received. I am keeping their letters for my next book!

I would also like to thank Jonathon Porritt, Anne Paintin, Liz Peltz from Friends of the Earth, Caroline Thomas, Dad, Mum, Jane Judd and all the correspondents for their encouragement, support and hard work, without which I wouldn't have had this opportunity to try to leave the world just a bit better than I found it.

The views and opinions expressed in this book are the authors' own, and do not necessarily reflect those of Friends of the Earth.

A Red Fox Book

Published by Random House Children's Books
20 Vauxhall Bridge Road, London SW1V 2SA

A division of Random House UK Ltd
London Melbourne Sydney Auckland
Johannesburg and agencies throughout the world

Copyright © Alex Johnston and Jonathon Porritt 1995
Copyright © illustrations McLachlan 1995
Copyright © fact boxes Friends of the Earth 1995

Copyright of individual letters rests with the individual author

1 3 5 7 9 10 8 6 4 2

First published in Great Britain by Red Fox 1995

Set in Bembo, Courier and Prestige Elite

Printed and bound in Great Britain by
The Guernsey Press Co. Ltd, Guernsey, Channel Islands

RANDOM HOUSE UK Limited Reg. No. 954009

Printed on 80 gsm Reece paper (50% re-cycled/50% Woodfree pulp)
Papers used by Random House UK Limited are natural, recyclable products made from wood grown in sustainable forests. The manufacturing processes conform to the environmental regulations of the country of origin.

ISBN 0 09 936041 1

Contents

Foreword

by Charles Secrett

Executive Director, Friends of the Earth

At Friends of the Earth our postbag is always bulging with letters from people who are worried about the environment. But it's an interesting fact that we receive more letters from children and young people than we do in any other age category!

Our young correspondents are very concerned about their world and one of the questions they often ask is 'what can I do to help?' Perhaps, as you're reading this book, this is something you've wondered about too.

If so, the answer is 'a lot'! Everyone has a part to play in caring for the environment. And the young have a particularly special role. After all, you're the ones who are going to be living in this world in the future – isn't it all the more important to have your say about how it's being looked after in the present?

In *Lifelines* you'll find out how one young person went about making her voice heard, through the power of the pen. Letter-writing is one of the simplest and most effective campaigning tools available to anyone. At the best, writing letters to people in power can help change the world. At the very least, it can be an educational and eye-opening experience!

But above all, letter-writing is one way that you can turn your concerns and fears into positive action and pressure for change. This is something that Friends of the Earth believes is absolutely vital if we are to solve the local, national and international environmental problems we all face. And it's exactly what Alex Johnston has done in this book. I hope it inspires you to think about the issues – and then pick up your own pen and have your say in the fight to protect *your* environment.

Introduction
by Jonathon Porritt

I started life as a teacher – ten years in a really good comprehensive school in West London. It was the kids in that school who really stirred up my interest in the environment; so much so that I gave up teaching to become Director of Friends of the Earth back in 1984!

For me, young people and the environment have always gone hand-in-hand. It is impossible for me to talk about 'the future' without thinking about the young people who will be inheriting that future. And part of the buzz I get from being a full time environmentalist is the thought that what I do matters as much for the time when I'll be dead and buried as I hope it does for today.

So it's not all that surprising that I ended up helping someone like Alex Johnston to do this book! I first got to hear of her (and her letter-writing) when two or three of the bigwigs she'd been bombarding with her ideas happened to mention her name to me. If she can make such an impact on that lot, I thought, there's got to be something special going on.

I wrote to her, and she immediately wrote back (Alex is brilliant at answering letters; I am absolutely hopeless!), we talked about her enthusiasm for all sorts of environmental issues, and eventually managed to meet up to talk about the idea of doing a book together with her writing all the letters and me editing the replies and putting them into some kind of order.

To be honest, I wasn't really sure that it would ever come to anything – until Red Fox surprised us both by saying they thought it was a great idea! So there we were in business.

It is worth saying a little about how the book finally emerged – if only because some people will suspect the worst. I *didn't* travel up and down to Northumberland pumping Alex full of all sorts of green propaganda which she then duly trotted out for public consumption. But we *did* talk about many environmental matters, I *did* send her stuff to read (most of which she thought was too 'boring' to dwell on for long!), and I *did* suggest some of the people she might like to write to. Which she then did with her own ideas in her own words.

To say that Alex has a mind of her own is something of an understatement. Whether it is parents, teachers or distant editors, she deals with them on her own terms. Here's how she explained her way of working with her father (who ended up typing out all her letters) to Phil Drabble. As one of her correspondents (see page 29) he'd asked her how she'd done it all!

> When we write 'talk 'n' type' letters, Dad just types and he hardly ever interrupts except when he thinks I'm being rude or something like that. If people think I'm saying what my Dad would like me to think, that's up to them. But they might as well say an *adult* author was just saying what somebody else wanted him/her to think. They would only say it because I'm a child, but that wouldn't make it true and it wouldn't be fair. I can think for myself just like anybody else can.

> I *want* other children to know that Dad typed my letters for me and explained complicated bits in all the leaflets I read before I wrote my essays, because then they could do what I am doing as well. It wouldn't be much fun if I didn't have anybody to discuss things with.

> One thing I have definitely learnt from my parents is you should never be afraid to say what you think. But I wouldn't dream of writing the sort of letters Dad writes, because sometimes he's incredibly rude to people. And then he's surprised when they don't answer! He's a bit of a hypocrite when I think about it, because he butts in if he thinks I'm being cheeky! Dad's completely mad – he's even writing that down and he's laughing about it! He wouldn't be a very good example for children at all, but I quite like him and he can type fast.

Perhaps Alex was being a little defensive about all this. Perhaps I am too! As it happens, I loathe the idea that adults might try to exploit children simply to advance their own cause, regardless of those children's own views. But I also believe very strongly that children *can* learn a lot from adults and that we constantly under-estimate their powers of thinking and their readiness to learn. That's what kept me on my toes for ten years as a teacher, and that's what I enjoyed so much rediscovering in Alex.

I am 44, Alex is just 13. I only wish I had felt as passionately about the environment at her age as she does today. It took me another ten years to wake up to the terrible things we were doing to the Earth and its creatures. So it was very good for me to meet someone who was almost *born* an environmental campaigner.

Reading through her letters and the answers to them, you may think it all looks rather easy. In fact, any budding letter-writer must expect a lot of disappointments in this area. Many of the people she wrote to couldn't be bothered to reply, and some just sent back the most formal and dismissive of letters. We haven't put those in the book because they were so boring. Alex never got depressed about this, and she was (to my way of thinking at least) unbelievably tolerant about some of the stuff she got sent.

But the whole thing has reinforced my belief in the importance of putting pen to paper and not just letting the world pass us by. There are so many cynics out there who believe that nobody ever listens, and so many indifferent slugabeds who would be hard put to stir themselves even if the sky fell in on them. So few people realize the impact that letters can have – especially when they come from young people.

If you don't believe me, write and ask the politicians for yourself! I will never forget John Gummer, Secretary of State for the Environment, rounding on a few of us environmentalists at the end of a rather strained meeting back in 1994, suggesting that it was *our* fault that the Government wasn't doing more to help protect the environment!

Why did he say it was our fault? Because we hadn't persuaded enough people to care enough about things to put more pressure on the Government. His evidence for this was the fact that MPs' postbags (all the letters they get in any one week) on environmental issues had fallen off since a peak of public concern in 1990.

Lots of letters equals (for politicians) an issue that can't be put off and has to be looked at. Only a few letters equals nothing very much to worry about. It may be a rather basic way of gauging public opinion, but politics is a pretty basic business.

Lifelines is only a very small contribution to solving a whole mass of very big problems. For me personally, it has been an inspiration to work with someone like Alex – not so much a question of me filling her with ideas, as she filling me with hope for the future.

Since Alex's Dad had to do all the typing (and refuses to use a computer!) it simply wasn't possible for him to do each letter individually. So Alex provided a standard letter, or essay, for each campaign, which was then sent to all her correspondents together with an individual covering letter. Still a lot of work, but manageable!

Chapter 1
FORESTS FOREVER

A lot of concern has been focused on the plight of the rain-forests over the last few years, and many of the big environ-mental organisations have made a real priority of this crucial international issue. But sometimes it seems as if it is *only* the rainforest that matters. In reality, of course, there are just as many problems affecting forest and woodlands in the UK and almost every country in the Northern Hemisphere. For exam-ple, there's pollution problems (such as acid rain), not enough trees being planted, or the wrong kind being planted, or woodland being cut down or not being properly looked after.

And that's the kind of thing Alex wanted to home in on in this letter – the first of her *Lifelines* campaigns.

Campaigning to preserve the world's shrinking rainforests is very important. But I think it is just as important, and maybe even more important, to set a good example here at home, and this does not seem to be happening.

A ruthless farmer in Britain who wants to chop down ancient trees because they are getting in the way of his tractors and harvesters can just destroy them, even if it means ruining a beautiful view for everyone else. The reason for chopping down trees in the rainforest is exactly the same - quick cash TODAY and never mind the consequences.

Anything which is old and beautiful and useful deserves respect, and destroying an ancient tree which is more useful alive than dead seems like killing a wise old man just to get his gold watch. The things the old man could have told you would be worth a lot more than his watch.

Besides producing oxygen, trees absorb

carbon dioxide, whereas people breathe oxygen and produce carbon dioxide. Trees can probably do without people, because there are plenty of other sources of carbon dioxide. But people cannot live without trees, so why are we destroying something we depend on?

People assume that the air we breathe has no value simply because we don't pay a penny for it. Actually there are people who plant trees just because they love and respect them, and I suppose you could say that these people work for us for nothing. People who live in the rainforests have respected the trees for thousands of years, and you could say that they have worked for us for nothing by preserving the forests. To me it seems unfair that we take all this for granted without giving anything in return, not even respect.

On the coast of Kenya, where I used to live, if there is someone in a village who wants to chop down a tree on his own land, a meeting is held, which is called a 'baraaza'. If nobody has any objection he can chop the tree down. But if just one villager decides that it makes good shade for cattle and goats on HIS land, then the tree won't be chopped down. This seems a very civilized arrangement to me. Sometimes there are other spiritual reasons for not cutting down a certain tree, which are always respected if somebody objects.

In India, they have another excellent tradition. When a baby is born a tree is planted and this is called a Birth Tree. When it is a sapling, the mother and father look after it, but when the baby grows into a child, then the child is encouraged to take an interest in it as well. If this tradition was taken up all over the world, then imagine how many trees we would have back. There is a baby born about every two seconds in the world, and soon everybody would have a personal interest in caring for at least ONE tree, which would be one more tree than a lot of people seem to care about now.

With the Government and environment organisations working together, it ought to be possible to organise a National Tree Planting Day to plant trees where they are most needed, beside roads. Every year certain roads could be closed down for one day and volunteers could come and plant seedlings which had been germinated by school children in warm classrooms or in warm kitchens at home.

You could really expand on the idea of a National Tree Planting Day, with a tree planting fund selling saplings of trees germinated by school children, tee-shirts and badges, etc, and the money raised could be used to send saplings of tropical trees, germinated by school children in Britain, to school children in Third World countries, together with plastic growing tubes to prevent them from being eaten by goats. It is easy to germinate avocados and mangoes, for example, from the stones, and I am sure there must be lots of exotic tree seedlings which children could germinate with easy instructions.

Most children in Britain do not care much about politics - why should they? They DO care about trying to help poor children who haven't got enough to eat and about looking after the environment. So even if adults thought a National Tree Planting Day was a boring waste of time (which most of them would!), children would just find adults who *did* care to make it work. Tree planting

13

picnics beside roads without any traffic whizzing past would be good fun.

One last point about barbecues. A lot of people in Third World countries are paid a pittance to go around destroying the little woodland they have left to make charcoal for people in Britain to use for barbecues. This seems ridiculous when we have millions of unemployed people of our own and millions of acres of crammed-together trees, fighting for light, which could be coppiced to make charcoal.

(Coppicing is when you cut down broad-leafed trees near to the ground and allow them to regenerate. When this has been done, a tree puts out as many as thirty new branches which can be chopped down again in twelve to fifteen years. A ton of charcoal sells wholesale for approximately £600.)

Why import charcoal from halfway around the world when we have all the raw materials on our own doorstep, and woodland which NEEDS to be coppiced?

Of course I care about the environment — this apron is made from recycled material.

When it came to thinking of people to send this to, where better to start than with James Lovelock, perhaps the leading independent scientist of his generation, author of a wonderful book about the nature of life on Earth (called *The Gaia Hypothesis* – which Alex gets to grips with later in her reply), and personally committed to 'restoring the balance' by establishing a small woodland at his own home in Cornwall.

Dear Alex,
Thank you so much for your letter and for your thoughtful essay on the rainforests.

I don't much enjoy reading letters because I receive too many and they are mostly dull or egomaniac. If I answered all of them there would be no time for work or pleasure. Your letter was an exception, well written and entertaining.

You are right about children having in some way more understanding than grown ups. A scientist who can't explain his ideas to an intelligent child probably does not understand them himself.

We are destroying the rainforests at a ruthless pace. We know it's wrong, but arguments for keeping the tropical forests are feeble; that they are the home of rare species of plants and animals, even of plants containing drugs that could cure cancer. They may do. They may even be slightly useful in removing carbon dioxide from the air. But they do much more than this.

By evaporating vast volumes of water vapour, and by making gases and particles that become the nuclei of cloud droplets, the forests serve to keep their region cool and moist by bringing the rain that sustains them. It is easy to calculate the value of the tropical forests from the energy that would be needed to provide the same air-conditioning and irrigating service - a service far more valuable than the use of the forest land for farming. It is worth about £10,000 per acre for tropical forests as a whole, that's about £300 trillion a year!

Yet every year we burn away an area of forest equal to the size of Britain, and often replace it with crude cattle farms. Unlike farms here in the temperate regions, the land of such farms rapidly becomes scrub or desert. When this happens the farmers fell more trees, and the burning away of the skin of the Earth goes on. Beyond a certain point the process becomes irreversible. When only 20 to 30 per cent of a tropical forest ecosystem remains, it can no longer sustain its climate and it collapses. At the present rate of clearance, it will not be long before the forests no longer have the critical mass they need to exist as self-sustaining ecosystems. When they vanish, the poor of those regions will be left with little to support them and in a harsher climate. This is a threat comparable in scale to a global nuclear war.

I'm sorry that this is a bit gloomy! If you have a more optimistic view of the future, hold on to it, and make sure it happens.

With best regards,

Jim Lovelock

Dear Mr Lovelock,

Thank you very much for your letter answering my essay on rainforests which I received in the post this morning. Your honesty about how you feel about getting letters which are either dull or egomaniac made me laugh. I will take a lot of trouble to try not to be dull or egomaniac in the future! A LOT of trouble!

What you seem to be saying is that governments and businessmen and scientists 'can't see the forest for the trees' and if they don't start looking at how the whole thing works, we haven't got a chance. And even if they do, perhaps we still haven't got a chance because it might be too late to do much about it.

That is a bit gloomy, I agree! But since writing to you, I've found out a little bit more about the 'Gaia' theory, that you wrote a book about. This seems to me to be much more hopeful. I must admit that I had never even heard of 'Gaia' so I looked it up in my dictionary. Apparently Gaia is the same as 'Ge', which means 'Personification of the Earth' and it comes from Greek mythology. Gaia was the Goddess of the Earth. So I *think* what you are saying is that the Earth is all one organism, and everything depends on everything else to keep it healthy. I agree with you (even if you are wrong!) because it's a good idea. If you could explain it so children can understand, you wouldn't have to explain it to grown-ups, because most children would agree with you anyway. It's obvious really.*

I think your Gaia theory is more important than just about anything else but hardly anybody knows about it. EVERYBODY ought to know about it.

With kindest regards,

Alex Johnston

---

* Alex was very keen that I should try and explain Jim Lovelock's Gaia Theory for all attentive readers. So I might have gone on about the Earth not being a lifeless lump of rock and soil, as most scientists would have us believe, but rather a *living organism*, with its climate and surface environment controlled by the plants and animals and bugs that inhabit it. But I won't, because *her* description is so much better!

Every year more than 12 million acres of tropical rainforest are logged for timber. Up to 50 wildlife species a day are becoming extinct due to rainforest destruction.

Giant trees up to 1,400 years old, wrapped in lichens and draped in mosses, are found in the temperate rainforests of Canada and the United States. Huge areas of these forests have been destroyed by timber and paper companies.

Richard Mabey is one of the best-known naturalists in the country, and writes for a host of magazines and newspapers on top of several books about the countryside and nature. But he is clearly somewhat less keen on encouraging young people to take up the cudgels in defence of the countryside, let alone to think of becoming authors themselves.

Dear Ms Johnston,
Many thanks for your letter. I wish I could reply at length, but I earn my living by writing, and just cannot spare that amount of time. But perhaps you will forgive me if I give you a few short reactions and words of advice.

I admire your enthusiasm, and your understanding of Third World attitudes towards trees, but not your suggestions for this country, I'm afraid. I think it would be very useful if you did a good deal more research and reading about what is happening already before chancing your arm on projects like this. One of the reasons well-intentioned green schemes don't get off the ground is because they are not always as well-informed as they should be.

Do you know the details of the dozen or so regional (and one national) community forests being created at present, which are likely to double the UK's tree cover over the next 50 years? Do you know the massive amount of planting the

Department of Transport (DoT) and the local authorities are already doing alongside roads? But are you also aware that planting alongside roads is in many ways the *worst* possible place to encourage trees, because of root vibration and disturbance, exhaust pollution, salt poisoning of roots, etc? And do you know that the most success-ful way of establishing woodlands is not by plant-ing but by allowing them to grow themselves (as they quickly will) on areas like set aside land?

With good luck and best wishes,

Richard Mabey

Sticks and stones may break my bones . . .

Dear Mr Mabey

I don't mind you criticising my ideas at all. In Kenya, when children ask adults about things they are interested in, adults go to a lot of trouble to explain the answers even when the children are somebody else's. It's the same in England, but you can't just go up to people you don't know, so you have to write to them instead.

The main 'green scheme' I've got is just to show other children that it's worth writing to people if you want to learn about something and find out if your ideas are any good. The more you learn about something, the more interesting it gets. One lady who is ninety-four writes to me whenever I write to her. She is in hospital because her body is worn out but her brain is excellent and she says she enjoys writing letters. All her letters are brilliant. If children knew about people like her I'm sure they would want to write to them as well, and they could learn a lot.

With best wishes,

Yours sincerely,

Alex Johnston

The UK is one of the world's largest consumers of timber. Each year we use about 25 million cubic metres, more than is used by the whole of India. As much again goes to produce our paper.

Only about 15 per cent of the timber and paper we use is produced in the UK. This makes us one of the largest importers of timber, wood pulp and paper from the forests of North America, Scandinavia and Europe, as well as from the tropical rainforests.

In Scandinavia, logging is the single largest threat to wildlife. Many hundreds of species face extinction.

However, it's only fair to say that Richard Mabey wasn't the only one to take Alex to task, especially about her comments on all those hateful vandals out there chopping down trees at every available opportunity. Michael Dower is the Director General of the Countryside Commission, and had some really helpful words of advice for Alex.

(It has to be said that he also charmed the socks off her by sending her an example of his 'fallen leaves card' – something so simple yet so inspiring that it had the whole Johnston family out there rummaging around amongst the autumn leaves!)

Dear Alex,

Thank you for your interesting essay and letter.

Like you, we think that there should be more trees in England. Twice as many in fact, and we would like these to be planted in the next fifty years or so. At the same time, we think it is very important that people should understand that once you have planted a tree, it needs to be looked after for a very long time; sometimes more than that person's lifetime. So we are very keen for people to think about how trees should be managed.

You mention that people can cut down trees in this country if they want to. This is not really true. Trees are protected in many ways, sometimes through Tree Preservation Orders, and sometimes through the Forestry Commission's system for controlling tree felling. No one can simply chop a mature tree down without permission.

Your idea about roadside picnics is interesting, but there might be some safety issues to resolve! The Department of Transport already does a great deal of roadside tree planting.

I think you have sent us some very good ideas and you should be pleased that people are already beginning to do some of the things you mention; of course, there is always plenty more to be done!

Your sincerely,

Michael Dower

PS By the way, have you ever thought of the idea of making your Christmas cards using the leaves that fall every autumn?

In Jersey, before any tree can be felled the case for cutting it down is heard in a special court where the tree is represented

Alex felt it was also important to write to some forestry experts, and homed in on Andrew Christie-Miller. He is the Chairman of the UK Timber Growers' Association, and has been at the forefront of building bridges between environmentalists and timber growers over the last few years.

Dear Alex,

Thank you for your letter and I certainly admire all that you are doing to campaign for the Environment. My reply follows the same paragraph order as your letter.

Paragraph 2: To say that a 'ruthless farmer can chop down ancient trees' is not true. In Great Britain we have a very strict set of rules and regulations controlling the felling and planting of trees. 'Favourite' trees in sensitive locations may also have Tree Preservation Orders (TPOs) placed upon them by the Local Planning Authority at the request of local people. In fact, we have one of the most highly-regulated forestry sectors in the world!

Paragraph 3: Ancient trees make an enormous contribution to the landscape. Dead trees can sometimes usefully be retained as they provide a host to a myriad of mosses, lichens and creatures great and small. However, we must be aware that trees have a finite life, and we should also be planting for their replacement for future generations.

The UK is a major importer of timber and timber products – currently about £7 billion per annum. We are one of the least afforested countries in the European Union and one of the largest consumers of forest products. It is right that we should 'respect' trees and seek to plant more trees to meet our requirements.

Paragraph 7: Planting trees to commemorate a birth is an excellent idea. I have a whole plantation in woods planted by my father when I was born. Likewise, it would be a good initiative for schools to adopt at a local level.

Paragraph 8: There already is a National

Tree Week to make people more aware of trees and the need for tree planting. It obviously needs more publicity if you haven't heard of it! There is also a scheme called 'Tree Aid' to help encourage tree planting in Third World countries.

Paragraph 11: Coppicing is only suitable for certain species of trees – namely hazel, ash, sweet chestnut and willow. It has been a dying art but recently it has gone through a revival in certain parts of the country, Hampshire, Wiltshire, Sussex, Kent. It is a very environmentally friendly practice and was how many of our woodlands were managed traditionally.

We have been investigating the charcoal market (for barbecues) for some time. We consume about 50,000 tonnes of charcoal annually in the UK but only about 6,000 is home produced. Some of the hardwood forests in the south east of the country would be particularly well suited to this process. I have a charcoal producer with his kilns operating in one of my own woods at this time.

I hope you will have got the impression from this letter that forest owners and timber growers in this country *do* respect trees. As you correctly point out we can hardly lecture the Brazilians, Indonesians or Russians about the sustainable management of their forests unless we are practising it ourselves. No one is perfect, but I believe we are setting a very fine example to other countries.

Best of luck with your endeavours!
Yours sincerely,

Andrew Christie-Miller

Dear Mr Christie-Miller,

Thank you very much for your excellent reply. I loved the way you answered each paragraph with your comments, because it shows that you took the trouble to think about what somebody else said as well as saying what *you* think about it.

I certainly did get the impression that 'forest owners and timber growers in this country *do* respect trees', and I got that impression from some of the other people who have written to me about it. It's nice finding out that so many important people *really do* want to leave the world better than they found it and they don't just talk about it, they are doing something about it. Newspapers and television pay too much attention to politicians and I think they ought to pay more attention to what ordinary people are doing, so children can understand that it's up to everybody and not just politicians to take care of our world.

Thanks too for the information about charcoal. There is a huge factory in Hexham called Eggar's which makes chip-board, so I expect they buy most of the wood which might be suitable for making charcoal, but I will try to find out. My best friend's Dad is called Roger McKechnie and he is the Chairman of the Acorn Trust, which has taken over sixty acres of derelict woodland from Consett Council. So I will get him on to all this charcoal business as I think he would be interested by it. (He already wants to start the idea of 'Birth Trees' on the land, which I am quite pleased about!)

One thing I thought might interest you is something I read in a newspaper: the Lord's Prayer has 58 words. The Ten Commandments have 297 words. The EC Directive on exporting duck eggs has 28,911 words!!!

Thanks again for the information.

With kind regards,

Yours sincerely,

Alex Johnston

Alex was also very pleased to hear from Andrew Christie-Miller that he was *already* using some of his woodlands for charcoal production. Just as she was getting her thoughts together about her woodlands campaign, she had come across an article in the *Telegraph* about the UK charcoal industry. At first glance, making charcoal might seem an extremely unfriendly environmental activity – and so it is, if it's done in the wrong way.

But if it is managed properly, it can be good for the environment *and* a good way for creating wealth. What the economists called a 'win-win' situation!

So Alex immediately wrote off to the author of the article, Gareth Huw Davies:

Dear Mr Davies,

In Kenya, where I used to live, African charcoal-burners were wrecking the countryside to sell charcoal to Saudi Arabia. All the top soil gets eroded and washes into rivers so the beaches get ruined as well and the sea gets muddy and spoils the coral. I expect it doesn't do the fish much good either!

You mentioned a new mobile kiln in your article. Do you think it might be better to make charcoal the way Africans do (just digging a hole in the ground and covering the wood up again with earth when it's started burning, and getting the charcoal out when it's ready) or would there be problems with that in Britain? But it would be cheaper than buying a mobile kiln for people who haven't got much money.

With best wishes.

Yours sincerely,

Alex Johnston

Dear Alex,

Thank you for your splendid essay on forests.
    There is clearly an enormous interest
among woodland owners to start charcoal
burning on their land - I know this from the
number of letters I received after writing
articles on the subject. There are a number
of mobile kilns being tested which will
enable charcoal burners to move freely about
the countryside to take advantage of the
available supply. There's no real need to
adopt the Third World 'pit kiln' option you
mention.
    People are still uneasy about changing
their consumer habits. But changing their
charcoal is such an easy move to make, and it
is immediately beneficial to the environment.
It is a superior consumer item too, easier
and quicker to light, better burning, and no
more expensive in the long run because you
don't need lighter fuel to get it going.
    And of course, it's safer. Last summer a
30-year-old woman in Bristol died from burns
after she poured methylated spirits on some
obviously inferior imported charcoal. So this
cheap stuff kills people as well as destroying the environment.
    I think you could help a lot by persuading
all your friends to insist that their parents
use British charcoal next summer, for *all*
these reasons.
    But I'm afraid too many of my generation
are either selfish or ignorant in continuing
their environmentally-destructive way of
life. They are very reluctant to change their
high-energy consumption habits, be it by buying low-energy bulbs, walking to the shops

instead of driving, or putting on an extra sweater instead of turning up the thermostat.

I wouldn't claim to be sky-high on green piety, but let me give you *one* example of how to work more efficiently by using public transport. I don't have a company car and I work more efficiently without one. I use the train a lot. I keep in touch by mobile phone and I work with a notebook computer on the train. Often I can manage three to four hours work. Any businessman could do this – save energy by using the train, and, thanks to new technology, be more productive. Then, as the railways become more profitable, they invest in a better service and attract more people to the railways. And so on!

Hope this helps!

Gareth Huw Davies

Dear Mr Davies,

Thank you very much for your interesting letter. Some of the ideas are really excellent, especially the way you use the train like an office and get such a lot of work done while you are travelling. Maybe it would be a good idea for British Rail to start a Business Class with fax machines and telephones and so on?

I was pleased that you liked my essay about protecting forests. The whole thing about children writing letters is that any child could get good answers as long as they read about the issues first. I read an article by Sir Laurens Van der Post where he said children should learn how to give as well as just getting, and I think it's a bit like that with letters.

With best wishes.

Yours sincerely,

Alex Johnston

Once felled, natural forests are often replaced by dense plantations to produce more timber than would occur naturally. However, these new 'factory forests' are of little value to wildlife or local inhabitants.

If harvested in a sustainable way, so that as many trees are planted as are cut down, and the forests' plants and wildlife are carefully protected, forests could provide both timber and a range of other benefits to society, *indefinitely*.

Alex has some very strong ideas about education – as you will see over the next few chapters! But one person who gave her an instant new angle on what education can mean, *in practical terms*, was Phil Drabble. His love of the land has been an inspiration to people for more years than most of us have been alive – and even now at the end of a wonderful career as a 'countryman', author and broadcaster, he is devoting his life to creating something for future generations.

Dear Alex,

Thank you for your interesting letter. I am most interested in the work you are doing and the possibility of a book, which I discussed on the phone with your father, and I will do all I can to help you make it a success.

My work here consists of managing habitat, as a game keeper would manage a shoot, not to produce a surplus of pheasants for sport, but to produce a surplus of certain special species of wildlife, which can overspill into the surroundings, where the public can enjoy them without threatening the reserve itself. There was a small heronry of 18 nests when I came in 1963, and this year they produced a record of 114, or more than 2 per cent of the national breeding population, proving my habitat management works!

But that's why there is no access to the wood - *except* for supervised visits by the children of the local village school, to whom my wife and I have dedicated it as an Educational Nature Reserve. For the *exclusive* use of these local children. We hope that we really are sowing the seeds for a more responsible future generation.

As a result of all this, I was the only private landowner in the country to receive a Joint Centre of Excellence Award, in partnership with Forestry Enterprise. Earl Howe, the Forestry Minister, was so impressed that he created a 'surprise' award, to be presented annually in future 'to the person deemed to have done most to arouse enthusiasm for trees and wildlife and commitment to the environment by the rising generation'. When he said this award would be known as the Phil Drabble Award for Commitment to Youth, it was the climax of my career.

I have now given up presenting programmes such as *One Man and His Dog* so that I can devote my whole energy to campaigning to prevent privatisation of the Forestry Commission or other exploitation of the countryside, both by writing and campaigning. As a youngster, who obviously feels strongly about such issues, you will be encouraged to learn what wide support I have received - and still do.

I hope that you will have great success with your book and as much pleasure as similar work has given me. 'Great oak trees out of little acorns grow', so remember that you *make* a great deal of your own luck and that it is sensible not to hide your light under a bushel because, if nobody knows you have written a book, they will not buy it!

Wishing you every species of good luck.

Phil Drabble

Dear Mr Drabble,

Thank you very much for your lovely letter, which arrived in the post this morning. I read it aloud to Dad and my sister on the way to school this morning and everybody thought it was wonderful. And the whole idea of the Phil Drabble Award for Commitment to Youth sounds brilliant.

The main thing I want to come out of my book is that leaving the world better than we found it is MUCH more important than getting more money than we need.

With best wishes.
Yours sincerely,

Alex Johnston

If there is one organisation that has been beating the drum for practical, local initiatives to get people more involved in their environment, it is Common Ground. Not for them the corridors of power in Whitehall or high level national campaigning, but rather the village green, the local high street and community woodlands.

PROPOSED SITE FOR NEW BRAIN

LOCAL PLANNING AUTHORITY

Dear Alex,
Thank you for your letter and essay. I am most impressed by the breadth of your knowledge and the care with which you have woven your ideas and arguments.

Common Ground is keen to help people recognise that everyone has a part to play - caring for the everyday environment - and to give them ideas to help get started. Tree Dressing Day for instance, is about celebrating our relationship with trees and going on to care for the mature trees on the green and in the street.

'Dressing' trees just means decorating them in some special way. It happens in all sorts of countries in all sorts of different ways!

When people do start getting interested, we have 15 tips on taking action:

31

(1) Water young or newly planted trees - at least a bucket a day during dry spells.

(2) Tell a neighbour how much you appreciate their garden trees.

(3) Ensure stakes and ties supporting newly planted trees are secure - but loosen ties if they are strangling a tree.

(4) Don't let builders stack heavy materials around the base of a tree as it will compact the earth and damage the roots and trunk.

(5) Always stop and ask questions if you see someone pruning or felling a tree. If you're not satisfied with the answers, alert the Tree Officer at the local council.

(6) Defend an old tree. Just because it's old and crooked, doesn't mean it's dying; it could go on living for centuries.

(7) Organise a tree walk in your parish or neighbourhood, to draw attention to your favourite trees and promote their importance.

(8) Become a Tree Warden.

(9) Get together and make a map of your favourite trees; send a copy to the parish, and District or Borough council.

(10) Don't chop any trees down when you move into a new house - you have a responsibility to the place you are moving to.

(11) Don't write-off a fallen tree; with just a quarter of its roots in the ground it can survive to be an interesting old character.

(12) Grow locally-native trees from seed.

(13) Start a tree nursery at school, home, office or factory.

(14) Make compost not bonfires.

(15) Plant the right tree in the right place.

Good luck with your project.
Yours sincerely,

Sue Clifford

We're just appreciating your apple trees, Mr Wenthorpe.

Dear Mrs Clifford,

Thank you very much for your fascinating letter.

Lord Allendale owns all the land around Bywell, where I live, and I think his family must have always loved trees. There is an oak tree outside the graveyard in a field, beside Bywell St Peter's church, with a metal plate fixed on the fence saying: *In commemoration of Queen Victoria's Jubilee 1887 Oak Tree planted by Miss Sophia Fenwick of Bywell Hall, 22 June 1887*. I expect everybody would have forgotten Sophia Fenwick by now, but her tree is about a hundred feet high. So even if she was not a very nice person she still left the world a bit better than she found it just by planting one tree!

I think planting a tree is the best thing people can do if they want people to remember them and think nice thoughts about them. I expect just about every tree has got a story which goes with it.

With kindest regards.

Yours sincerely,

Alex Johnston

TIME FOR ACTION!

Gareth Huw Davies put his finger on it:

> 'I think you could help a lot by persuading all your friends to insist that their parents use British charcoal next summer.'

50,000 tonnes of charcoal are used on barbecues every year. Only 6,000 tonnes of that is produced here at home – all the rest is imported, often from countries which are suffering very badly from cutting down the trees in order to make the charcoal.

So, first you need to persuade your parents – just give them the facts!

All they then have to do is to ask for British charcoal in whatever DIY store or garage they buy their charcoal from.

Make sure they are not brushed off by somebody who doesn't know anything about it – just ask to see the manager!

And simply don't believe them if they claim that British charcoal isn't available: that just means they haven't been trying hard enough!

But *always be polite and constructive*.

Apart from careful charcoal buying, the other action points we might suggest are all summed up brilliantly in Sue Clifford's letter.

From trees and woodlands to weeds and farmland – time to take on the dreaded Common Agricultural Policy!

Chapter 2
FARMING FOLLIES

The Common Agricultural Policy (CAP) is probably the most important of all the European Union's policies.

It has been around a long time now, having been thought up after the Second World War as the best way of ensuring that each country in Europe would be able to produce as much of its own food as possible. Basically it's an attempt by the European politicians to control what goes on in farming. It offers subsidies for certain crops or farms and controls what can be grown.

Whether you're talking cows, corn, sheep or peas, the CAP has a finger in every pie!

The funny thing is, it's worked too well! Farmers were given such huge subsidies that the biggest problem the CAP faced at the end of the 1980s was surpluses – too much food was being produced. And very serious damage was being done to the countryside and to Britain's flora and fauna in the process.

All sorts of different ways have been tried to reduce these surpluses, including paying farmers less and making them take up to 15 per cent of their land out of production altogether, i.e. letting the land just lie unused, and being given a subsidy to do so – the so-called 'set aside' scheme.

As a result, the food mountains that Alex finds so offensive (see overleaf) have begun to decline. But for how long will that last? What's going to happen when all those countries in Eastern Europe (like Poland, Hungary and Czechoslovakia) eventually join the European Union?

Has the CAP had its day altogether? That's certainly Alex's view.

It used to be a dormouse

CAP

(after JT)

However hard I try to make sense of the Common Agricultural Policy (CAP) the whole thing seems as much like crazy nonsense as the Mad Hatter's tea party in Alice in Wonderland. How can it be a good thing to wreck our countryside, kill off all the wildlife, ruin the soil and poison people? 'Ah!' says the Mad Hatter. 'You're just a little girl, Alice, so OF COURSE you don't understand. Wait until you are grown-up and THEN you will see that it all makes perfect sense.'

If a farmer has a farm with beautiful hedgerows and woods, and masses of wildlife, and he loves the land and everything about it, that farmer would obviously look after it. A 'big-business farmer', on the other hand, who only cares about money, would want to squeeze every penny out of every inch of land that he could get his hands on. So if the Government comes along and says it will

pay farmers extra cash if they grow more
wheat, for example, the big-business farmer
will think nothing of destroying all his
woods and hedgerows to make one big field,
which will be easier to plough, plant and
harvest, and then drenching the empty landscape with weedkillers and insecticides and
fertilizers to get a bumper crop.

The 'care-taking farmer', who loves his
land will have a terrible choice of either
doing the same thing and feeling like a
vandal, or growing things which makes less
free money from the Government, and maybe
going broke in the end and having to sell his
farm to the big-business farmer who will
wreck everything that the good farmer was so
proud of. So that the good farmer might just
as well have wrecked it himself and got rich
on free money. Anybody can see that isn't
fair. It is a poisonous idea, including
poisoning a good farmer's feelings of
responsibility for his land.

The end result is 'wheat mountains' and
'butter mountains' and 'wine lakes' and 'beef
mountains' and so on, and sometimes farmers
even being paid to plough crops back into the
ground because there isn't anywhere to store
them, which does seem really wicked when you
think of all the people in the world who are
starving because they can't even grow enough
food to survive. While civilised people are
giving money to Oxfam, Save the Children,
etc, their taxes are being used to plough
food back into the ground.

You would think that all this muddle would
be enough to worry even the Mad Hatter. But
instead of saying 'Oh dear! Let's think about
this again right from the beginning', politicians tinker about with the muddle and make

it even worse - as with 'set aside'. Set aside means farmers are paid to grow nothing at all on a chunk of their land, so that they produce less. No more food mountains, lots of uncultivated land for wildlife, and everybody can relax again. That's the theory.

Well, it doesn't work. As soon as a piece of 'set aside' land starts to go back to nature, with no chemical rubbish being dumped on it, there is an explosion of ragwort which can kill horses, and other 'pernicious weeds' which can quickly spread if they are not controlled. So farmers plough it all up at the end of the year and set aside another piece of land to get another dollop of free money. Then they look around for stronger chemical fertilizers and weedkillers and more efficient machines to make up for lost ground, and end up producing even bigger crops than they were getting before.

Even the care-taking farmers can't afford not to take some free money for set aside. I know that I would take free money not to grow crops on a piece of land where probably I didn't want to grow them anyway. Wouldn't you?

Some farmers get so depressed at all this they end up killing themselves, and lots of them go bankrupt. What could be more disgusting than driving good farmers to despair just because they want to be responsible care-takers of the land?

Other farmers have learnt how to beat the crazy system. One farmer discovered, for example, that instead of making a 'scorched earth' border with expensive weedkiller all around his crops to stop weeds from encroaching, it only cost a little bit more to sow a border of thick grass and wild flowers which would bomb out any weeds which tried to grow. Every time he did it, the cost was less and less, because the grass and wild flowers had got well established. In the long run, it was actually cheaper and, of course, the border became a chemical-free sanctuary for wildlife and for insects who helped to pollinate the crops and eat all the other insects.

Lots of farmers say they hate getting money for nothing because it takes away their pride and dignity and forces them to behave like swindlers, taking tax-payers' money and giving nothing back. So why not use the money for things that tax-payers and responsible farmers DO want?

The Government knows very well what tax-payers and good farmers want, which is environment-friendly farming, better animal welfare, more help for small farmers and organic farmers, etc, so why not? Even Screaming Lord Sutch, who is the leader of the Monster Raving Loony Party, has more sensible ideas than the Common Agricultural Policy, and there must be SOME politicians who are more sensible than Screaming Lord Sutch. As the saying goes, 'the lunatics are taking over the asylum'. But when the whole wide world is the asylum, where can the sane people go?

'Now, now, Alice!' says the Mad Hatter, 'there's no need to get cross! Everything will be all right, you'll see!'

'I hope that it will be', says Alice, 'but you seem to have gone a curious shade of green!'

Alex didn't want to send this letter to environmentalists or people with little knowledge of the countryside. She wanted to find out from *farmers* what they thought of her ideas.

So the first in her sights was Robin Page, presenter of *One Man and His Dog*, a Cambridgeshire farmer, and well-known for his passionate concern for the countryside in that rather denuded part of the world.

Dear Alex,

Thank you very much for your letter which I found extremely amusing and perceptive. If only you were Minister of Agriculture, Britain's countryside would be so much better!

My views are very simple. I believe, that set aside was a wasted opportunity, and that if less production was wanted (to reduce surpluses), then there ought to have been controls put on the use of fertilizers.

A sensible system of *mixed* farming (crops and livestock) would, I believe, have provided the agricultural answers as well as the environmental solutions. From this it will be obvious that I think the present payments are absolute nonsense. As you say, it means the rich irresponsible farmer just gets richer, and I do not believe that any Government or CAP handout should be made to a farmer without strong environmental conditions.

So stick with it!
With best wishes.

Robin Page
Chairman – Countryside Restoration Trust

Dear Mr Page,

Thank you very much for your letter. I don't think I would be a very good Minister of Agriculture, though, because politicians are terrified to say anything at all in case they mess up their chances. I don't think they *really* believe in freedom of speech!

For instance, if you write to a Minister, your letter has to go to a lot of people, one by one, and they have to make little notes on it with advice and suggestions before he is allowed to answer himself.

Your letter makes complete sense to me, so I expect it wouldn't be nearly complicated enough for the European Union or the Ministry of Agriculture. Trying to understand what they're on about is a bit like learning a foreign language.

With best wishes.

Yours sincerely,

Alex Johnston

Since the 1940s we have lost at least 95% of our flower-rich meadows, 50% of our ancient woodlands and 50% of our fens and wetlands. Over 368,000 kilometres of hedgerows have been dug up.

Over 200 of our most important areas for nature conservation – Sites of Special Scientific Interest – are damaged or destroyed each year. At the current rate, 50% of all Sites of Special Scientific Interest could be damaged or destroyed by the end of the century.

In 1990, a Government survey revealed an alarming loss of habitats and wildlife species since 1978 in more than 1,000 sites throughout the countryside.

Her next correspondent was even more emphatic. Matt Ridley is a partner in a mixed dairy/arable farm in Northumberland, not so very far from where Alex herself lives. He is also a journalist on the *Telegraph*, with a well-earned reputation for stirring the pot and occasionally putting the boot in!

Dear Alexandra,

Thank you for your letter. I agree with you that the Common Agricultural Policy is mad, bad and foolish. The adult world, you will find if you keep your mind open, is full of things that are mad and achieve the opposite to what was intended, but are defended by long established special interests.

To argue that British farmers would be better off without government subsidy - and without government control - is like eating a pork chop in a mosque. Most farmers act as if the subsidy they receive is not only vital to their survival, but is their due - compensation in some way for being at the whim of the weather and unfair foreign competition.

What would happen if the CAP were abolished overnight? There would be a big saving to the tax-payer and a fall in food prices across the board. Countries such as Holland and Britain, with their modern machinery, would have little trouble increasing their market share. Those, such as hill farmers, whose enterprises aren't very efficient even with subsidy, could still be supported by more targeted payments.

Above all, farmers would be free to make their own decisions.

Your letter doesn't really take into account the way in which farming is effectively being 'nationalised' by politicians. Half a century ago a farmer was entirely free to choose what to grow. Now he may only milk cows if he has a quota (a set number or share), licensed by the Ministry, and he may only sell his grain if he has satisfied the bureaucrats in the Ministry that the acreage he has planted is exactly that which they have agreed to, down to the last minute detail. He may only keep beef cattle or hill sheep if he has quotas, passports and other forms of centralised 'permission'.

We have slipped gradually into a system in which our countryside is run not by the people who know it and live on it, but by bureaucrats in the national Ministries and in Brussels who take centralised, unchallengeable decisions and dictate them down to farmers. This worked very poorly in Russia, and it is working very poorly here.

The Common Agricultural Policy is the worst form of foolish central planning. It is this, not the greed of farmers, that results in environmental damage by farming. It's an ideal time to begin to dismantle the whole apparatus of farm subsidy. It has done nothing but harm to the industry and the countryside. Must we always keep a hold of nurse for fear of finding something worse?

Yours sincerely,

Matt Ridley

Dear Mr Ridley,

Thank you very much for your fascinating letter. I read that people in China only pay doctors if they don't get ill, so maybe we should only pay politicians if they don't cause any problems by making new laws all the time. I read a lot of really boring leaflets about the CAP and set aside before I wrote my essay about it, and everybody except politicians thinks that the CAP is completely crazy. But obviously you have thought about it more than I have, so now I'm *convinced* it's crazy.

All the people who really know anything are people like you, and all the people who are useless seem to become MPs, which is the wrong way round. I don't know how we could change that, unless people like you become MPs. But you probably wouldn't want to or you would have already done it!

       With best wishes.

       Yours sincerely,

           Alex Johnston

Soil erosion due to intensive farming has become a growing threat, particularly in the South Downs, the Fens, North Norfolk and the Vale of York. The Soil Survey of England and Wales reported in 1988 that 44% of the country's farmland was at risk from erosion.

The disposal of liquid and animal waste (or slurry) from intensive livestock farming can seriously harm rivers and streams. In one case, 30,000 fish died when slurry spilled into a stream.

Between 1964 and 1989 the number of farm holdings in the UK fell from 445,000 to 252,000. Over 8,000 people have left farming every year over the past decade. Just over 1% of the British workforce is now employed in agriculture.

Doing away with the CAP sounds fine but what kind of farming should we be encouraging in the meantime? What about organic farming, for instance, which uses *no* artificial chemicals?

Alex reckoned she might as well have a crack at one of the best known organic farmers in the land: His Royal Highness the Prince of Wales. He feels so strongly about the problems of modern farming that he converted his estate at Highgrove into an organic farm in the early 90s.

Alex was very pleased to get a personal reply.

Dear Alexandra,

Thank you so much for the letter you sent me some months ago and for sending me your critique of the Common Agricultural Policy. It makes interesting reading and I certainly agree with you about the problems of set-aside. It definitely goes against the grain (!), as far as I am concerned, and I long for the day when a workable policy can be found which will allow land to be kept in production, but less intensively, and which will also allow lost habitat to be re-created all over the UK - so that we have more room for wildlife and a more attractive countryside.

At Highgrove we are trying an experiment with organic farming - which means not using any chemical fertilisers or pesticides at all. This is, after all, how people farmed for many hundreds of years, with great success, and is, in my opinion, a truly sustainable form of agricultural management. We have cattle (both beef and dairy), sheep and a range of arable crops. Because we don't use any chemicals the land produces smaller harvests than other farmers can achieve (though not all that much smaller now that things are settling down) but people are prepared to pay higher prices for crops which are certified as organic, so we do still make a profit. We have even started a company making biscuits from the organic oats and wheat, and I am enclosing two packets for you to try!

I hope this answers at least some of your questions, but if you would ever like to look around the farm - and the garden - for yourself, do let me know. You might find it interesting!

Yours sincerely,

Charles

But what of the men from the Ministry, the guests at the Mad Hatter's tea party? After all, they're the ones holding the purse strings and pulling the levers of power – when Brussels will let them, that is. Alex prefaced her letter to William Waldegrave, the Minister himself, with the following comment:

When Mr Major made you the new Agriculture Minister and put you in charge of the Common Agricultural Policy in Britain, I expect you must have been horrified. Being a farmer yourself, you probably agree with a letter I received this morning, which was from a farmer who said, 'the Common Agricultural Policy is mad, bad and foolish'. It must be very difficult when you are put in charge of something like that. So I hope you will not think I am getting at you because I know you haven't had time to change anything yet. It would be lovely if you could write to me and let me know if there is anything good about the CAP, in your opinion, because so far every letter I get makes it seem worse than the last one did!

Alex first got a reply from John Flowerdew (whose name alone must make him stand out in the barren wastes of the Ministry of Agriculture!) and then from the Minister, William Waldegrave. He has only just been promoted to the job, and is raising high hopes amongst environmentalists that he might be just the one to sort out the CAP fiasco and do wonders for environment-friendly farming in the process. Judge for yourself.

Dear Miss Johnston,

May I first of all say that your paper is very well thought out but, if I have a criticism of it, it would be its reluctance to recognise the fact that there are two sides (at least) to every story.

To understand the 'success' of the CAP, it is necessary to go back to a period way before you were born. The CAP was first con-ceived during the years following the Second World War, a time when the land was devastated and food was in short supply. The whole idea was to introduce an agriculture system which would never again allow people to go short of food. In those terms, the CAP has been a remarkable success. However, the world has moved on and the problem now is not one of food shortage but one of food surplus.

On the whole, farmers *do* look after the land. There is no link as you suggest, between the destruction of the countryside and big business farmers. Small farmers may be under *more* pressure to increase yields as they have less land, whilst large-scale farm-ers can often be environmentally friendlier because they have the resources.

You quote the Mad Hatter advising Alice that there is no need to get cross about the state of affairs. However, it *is* sometimes necessary to get cross to ensure that things we value are protected. The Government has fought very hard within the European Union to bring about development of the CAP to address environmental issues.

Which is why this Ministry has introduced a package of schemes to encourage farmers to manage their land in an environmentally friendly way. These have included the Environmentally Sensitive Area scheme (areas of outstanding nature conservation, landscape and historic interest where farms are offered payment to manage their land in various traditional ways), a new Habitat Scheme (offering payments to farmers to promote nature conservation on their farms by taking carefully selected areas of land out of production for 20 years and managing them in environmentally beneficial ways), a new Nitrate Sensitive Areas Scheme (which will help protect selected ground water sources to supply drinking water), and an Organic Aid scheme to help farmers wishing to convert to organic methods of production. Very shortly we will also be launching a Countryside Access Scheme to increase opportunities for public access to set aside land.

Taken together, these schemes represent a substantial commitment to environmentally sensitive farming. Once they are all fully operational, Government spending on environmental schemes will have risen from nothing to over £110 million in 10 years.

I hope the above adds to your understanding of the issues involved in respect of agricultural policy.

Yours sincerely,

John Flowerdew

Dear Miss Johnston,

The main thing I would add to John Flowerdew's reply is that it is impossible to have a Europe in which goods are freely traded without each country having to do some things which it doesn't much like.

For example, we will never get the Spanish and the Italians to treat their animals better unless they are compelled to do so under CAP rules. It is a bit like environmental campaigning: if we are going to make our farmers keep their hedges, it is a bit unfair for them to have to trade with other people who are not doing so. So *common action* in a lot of these areas is very sensible.

Sometimes, however, it means that we have to accept things *we* don't much like. Many of our farmers, for example, don't like set aside. (I am not sure, actually, that they would much like the alternative either which is lower prices for their products so that less is produced.) So we have to put up with it.

Meanwhile, I am trying to get useful things done with set aside, like having trees planted on it.

With all best wishes.

Yours sincerely,

William Waldegrave

Dear Mr Waldegrave,

Thank you very much for your letter. Judging by what you say, I think you will have to be extremely tough insisting that British farmers must be allowed to do whatever is best for Britain. If other European countries want to chop down all their hedges, destroy all their wildlife, pay their farmers for not growing anything on set aside, etc, etc, and end up living in a desert, then that should be up to them. WE all have to live in Britain, not in other European countries.

Another problem is other countries in Europe cheating all the time, while Britain is doing its best to obey the laws. The more I hear about the huge swindles in Brussels, the more I believe that CAP really stands for Crime Against the Planet! So it must be better to have laws which suit US, and let other European countries have laws which suit THEM. Italy is completely different from Britain, so I can't see any way that we could have laws for farmers which suit Italy AND Britain. It would be like saying that the Italian climate has to be the same as the British climate, and Italian farmers have to be honest like British farmers.

I am only thirteen, so I don't have your experience of life yet, but things like that are obvious to everybody even if they are only ten! You are clearly an extremely intelligent person, so I can't see how you wouldn't agree that it's just IMPOSSIBLE. And that's all there is to it!

With best wishes.

Yours sincerely,

Alex Johnston

Mr Flowerdew's letter (what you are seeing is a very much shorter version of the original!) gave Alex material to be chewing on for weeks.

(He might just have mentioned, by the way, that the £110 million for environmental-friendly schemes which he refers to at the end of his letter, is still only a very small fraction of the £3 billion or so spent on agriculture every year.)

At least they are *all* on board a slightly greener agricultural bandwagon in one way or another. You might even think from the next letter that Sir David Naish, President of the NFU, had built that bandwagon with his own bare hands!

Dear Alex,

Thank you for your letter. I think it's only fair to point out that the countryside has been shaped and managed for hundreds of years to produce the kind of countryside that is now treasured by so many. For many it is a place of rest and relaxation; for farmers, however, the countryside is still the workplace from which they must derive their living.

The central question now facing all of us as we approach the end of the present century is how the British countryside can retain its attractions while still meeting the need to grow and provide food.

Many farmers *are* concerned about their ability to continue to plant new hedgerows and woods, or restore farm ponds, in a situation where there may be less labour and financial support to undertake these tasks. The point is that farming businesses *have* to be profitable to produce the resources with which to manage the countryside. That is why the NFU has called for a comprehensive (but still *voluntary*) conservation scheme available to all farmers and growers across Britain.

Modelled on the existing Environmentally Sensitive Area Scheme (ESA), it would be based

on a plan covering the *whole* farm and lasting
from five to ten years. It would amount to a
contract to supply *both* food *and* environmental
benefits. That's very much in line with what you
were saying in your letter about using public
money for things the public clearly want. But
on the other hand, we cannot expect our farmers
and growers to become mere 'park keepers'.

The Government, farmers, and others involved
in the countryside must now work together to
achieve these objectives, each understanding
the others' needs and concerns. Only in this
way will we be able to produce and manage the
countryside that future generations will regard
with affection.

Yours sincerely,

David Naish

One organisation that has really begun to pick up the
challenge of 'stewardship in the countryside' is the Country
Landowners Association (CLA). So the letter from George
Dunn (their Rural Economic Advisor) was eagerly awaited.

Dear Alex,

Thank you for your very interesting letter. Farmers often bear the brunt of public criticism, and I have to say that a lot of this has been unfair. Farmers have simply been responding to the economic signals they have been receiving, as would any other rational human being. If someone indicated that they would be willing to offer you £50 for every essay you produced, I am sure that you would spend most of your spare time trying to produce as many essays as possible!

If blame is to be placed anywhere, it should be at the door of those giving the economic signals. If farmers and landowners receive the correct signals from policy makers, they will be better placed to respond.

You also make some comparisons between 'big business' farmers and other farmers. The situation is *not* as clear cut as you suggest. In fact, big farms can offer major environmental benefits which small farms cannot.

Currently in the UK, the Common Agricultural Policy provides £3 billion for the rural areas, though not all of this goes into the pockets of farmers. An overnight removal of this money would have serious consequences for the rural economy and rural environment.

I wish you every success in your research. You certainly already have a wide knowledge of the subject and your enthusiasm is infectious! I think what you are doing is tremendous and I hope that it proves an inspiration to other young people to make their views known. As Paul said to Timothy (1 Timothy, Chapter 4, Verse 12), *'Don't let anyone look down on you because you are young, but set an example for the believers in speech, in life, in love, in faith and in purity.'*

With best wishes.

Yours sincerely,

George Dunn

PS I will be very pleased to receive a copy of your book once it is published.

Dear Mr Dunn,

Thank you very much indeed for going to so much trouble to explain what the Country Landowners Association's position is concerning the CAP. Where you say 'if blame is to be placed anywhere, it should be at the door of those giving the signals', I think you have hit the nail right on the head!

    With best wishes.

    Yours sincerely,

       Alex Johnston

PS I loved the quotation from 1 Timothy, which I hadn't seen before, but I think it is better in the unmodernised Bible which I looked up. The new version seems to have changed the meaning a bit. The old one says 'be thou an example of the believers (ie Christians), in word, in conversation, etc.' but the new version talks about people who believe in speech, in life, in love, etc, which isn't really the same thing. I suppose modern language is easier to understand, but I think Muslims are right when they say the original Holy Koran ought to be left alone and not changed. It must be very difficult not to change the meaning when words are changed, and the language in the James Bible is beautiful even if it sometimes isn't very clear what it means. That's my opinion, anyway, and I expect it isn't politically correct. I hope so. ('Through a glass darkly' is as clear as mud, but it sounds lovely, doesn't it? It would be a shame to ruin it.)

In 1989 a *Daily Telegraph*/Gallup Poll on farming and the countryside found that:

62% thought farmers should produce the same amount of food as at present but using more land and less fertilisers.

75% believed the Government should discourage farmers from using fertilisers. A similar number said they would be willing to pay more for food if it meant fertilisers being used less frequently.

By this stage, Alex had readily accepted all the things she had
left out in her original essay, including the importance of a
historical perspective, and the impressive success of modern
farming, etc, etc. But she still had no real sense that the policy
makers knew what they were doing or where the CAP was
going in the future.

And the letter from Rene Steichen, the EU Commissioner
himself (*the* top man), the man responsible for the day to day
running of the CAP and its future reform, did little to dispel
that impression.

Dear Miss Johnston,
I read your essay with interest. I was however very
concerned about your criticism of the Common
Agricultural Policy. Security of food supply is the
key issue which you've ignored. When it was set up
in 1962, the aim of the CAP was to make sure food
was always available for EC consumers at affordable
prices, while ensuring farmers a fair income for
their efforts. The CAP has fulfilled that principal
task. The Community is more than self-sufficient in
nearly all major products.

However, in recent years it became clear that the
CAP was in need of change. Technology enabled farmers
to increase yields, causing surpluses in areas like
cereals, beef and milk. As a result, a lot of money
was spent on selling off surpluses at subsidized
prices on the world market. The cost of the CAP
increased, but farmers' income did not. Consequently
the EC decided to update the CAP in 1992. The aim of
this new policy is to stabilize production at a level
more in line with current demand.

I notice that your essay mainly reflects the views
of individuals on the CAP. Perhaps I can take this
opportunity to supply you with some of the *facts*.
The reforms are already achieving the most important
objective of reducing production. The Commission's
latest estimate of the 1993 harvest is 163 million
tonnes, 17 million tonnes lower than it would have

been without set aside and other changes. The cereals 'mountain' has been reduced from more than 30 million tonnes (in 1993) to approximately 15 million (current stocks) and looks set to reduce still further in the future.

I hope, as you do, to encourage farmers to remain on the land, and to protect the environment. Additional measures *have* been introduced to finance the development of more environmentally friendly types of agriculture (with less pesticides and fertilisers). These schemes are very similar to the programmes you suggest in *your* essay.

Yours sincerely,

Rene Steichen

As Alex said in her reply:

'I think it is a very good sign that an EC Commissioner would bother to answer my essay about the CAP because it shows you will listen. You went to a lot of trouble to write me an excellent letter and I really appreciate that.'

But one can't help thinking that the reason more answers weren't forthcoming from the experts in this exchange is simply that the answers require so radical a re-think that it's just easier to muddle along with what we've got. However awful it may be. This was confirmed by a letter from an old friend of Alex's father. Dor Bertram is 94 years old, an ardent letter-writer even now, and bright as a button. Of all the replies Alex got for this book, this is one of her absolute favourites.

My dear Alex,
What a surprise – your most interesting letter and enclosed draft. I had heard from your Granny you were writing it, but it is so well put together and you have such a grasp of the CAP – *far* better than I! Amazing at your age – which is what – 12?

I quite agree, 'Set Aside' is a terrible idea – but up here the farms are not really affected as they are mostly *hill* farms – who don't grow crops – just enough for their own use. As the grazing is not so good they get a subsidy from the Government for a certain number of animals – Tony (my son) has about 1200 sheep, 800 lambs, about 800 cattle I think, and 2 bulls.

He is mostly affected by the *vast* number of forms which have to be filled in for everything and wastes *hours* of time. Also all the fields had to be measured again with a new map (which cost £30!).

Tony has a computer and is intelligent but he finds it difficult – and there are lots of old farmers who can't cope and have to pay for someone to help them. They had a meeting of farmers lately – 2 Men from the Ministry to show them – and *they* couldn't answer some questions!

We had a Home Farm at my old home near here, and I remember a lovely Jersey herd and bull - always luscious cream and butter - cattle and sheep - and I can't remember a Vet ever coming. Cattle were not destroyed for Foot-and-Mouth and if they recovered, were very healthy. Now animals - especially sheep - get most odd diseases. Poor Tony is always having the Vet, but the new drugs seem very effective. He runs a very efficient farm, and the animals are well cared for, but the germs still seem to come - and new unknown ones. He took one cow - and later a sheep - in to the Veterinary College in Edinburgh, and *they* didn't know! They have kept the cow for observation.

A Common Agricultural Policy is quite a mad idea, as every country has different way of life - different habits, climate, etc. I am sure NONE of the old, illiterate French or Italian farmers will comply - they like things *their* way. French farmers are much more vociferous than ours - blocking roads - letting British sheep out of their lorries if they are objecting to some new rule.

Best of luck with your book.

Dor

As both Alex and William Waldegrave have pointed out, everything gets even more complicated when a policy has to be agreed by every single country in the European Union before anything can happen. Exactly the same sort of muddle seems to be looming with the EU Ecolabelling Scheme, the subject of the next chapter. But first . . .

TIME FOR ACTION!

A lot of people don't think much about where the food they're eating comes from. Apart from what's sold in a few farm shops or shops that make a point of stocking *local* produce, most of our food goes through the big retailers' distribution systems to end up on those well-stocked supermarket shelves.

Environment organisations have been advising people for a long time that they can really help here by buying *locally* and by buying *seasonally* – that's to say, when a fruit or vegetable is in season – rather than buying stuff which is shipped or flown in from around the world just to give us all 'more choice'.

It's now possible to go a bit further – by buying *directly* from the farmer, cutting out all the middle men along the way, and by buying organic produce. There are now dozens of these direct sales schemes around the country, delivering to your door, at prices which mean that organic food will cost you very little more than the usual fruit and veg you'd be buying at the supermarket.

For further details, just contact the Soil Association at 86 Colston Street, Bristol BS1 5BB, tel 01179 290661, and they'll send you a really helpful leaflet called *Linking Farmers and Consumers: How you can support local farms and eat fresh organic foods.*

If you're getting inspired by all this letter-writing, you might like to write to William Waldegrave, the Agriculture Minister, to let him know what *you* think about the CAP.

And why not set out to encourage him rather than criticise him! You may not believe it, but politicians need a lot of encouragement, and Mr Waldegrave really is trying to help get some of the worst bits of the CAP sorted out.

In December 1994, for instance, he managed to persuade his fellow Ministers in Europe that it would be far more sensible to allow farmers to plant trees on set aside land rather than do absolutely nothing with it. This is by no means the whole solution to the 'Mad Hatter policy of Set Aside', but it's certainly an improvement.

Ministers are always astonished when they get letters complimenting them on something that they've done. You may even persuade them to go on and do the next thing!

Chapter 3
CRUELTY TO LABELS

Like many young people, Alex cares passionately about animals. She simply can't understand how 'the adult world' seems perfectly happy to go on abusing and torturing animals in the name of what it calls 'progress'.

In 1992, over 2.9 million experiments were carried out on animals in British laboratories. These experiments involved animals being poisoned, starved, blinded, deprived of water, subjected to electric shocks, used in operations and infected with dangerous diseases. In two-thirds of these experiments no anaesthetic was used. At the end of most experiments the animals used are killed. Worldwide it is estimated that over 100 million animals are used in laboratories every year.

That's one of the reasons Alex has always been such an admirer of Anita Roddick and The Body Shop, whose campaigning against the use of experiments on animals in the cosmetics industry has done much to alert people's attention to the whole issue of animal testing. So when she heard that Anita Roddick was threatening to boycott the newly-launched Ecolabelling Scheme, precisely because of its failure to address animal welfare issues, that was more than enough to trigger her campaigning instincts! The first thing she did was to find out more about the Ecolabelling Scheme – and the part it plays in the whole Green Consumer movement.

So far so good, but as Alex has discovered on other issues, nothing in the EU is as simple as it sounds! Particularly when it comes down to different ideas about animal welfare. This is the letter she prepared to try and get to the bottom of a complex issue – and to find out from animal welfare organisations and from members of the Ecolabelling Board here in the UK why they aren't able to agree on something that seems to her so *obvious*.

According to opinion polls, around 50 per cent of the British public choose to buy one product over another because they think it is better for the environment.

'Green' claims on products can be misleading. In one case, a car manufacturer claimed its car was 'ozone friendly' because it ran on unleaded petrol – not mentioning that lead has no effect at all on the ozone layer!

The opinion polling organisation Mintel reported in 1991 that 63 per cent of people questioned were 'confused' about green claims.

The eco-label, an official green labelling scheme for Europe, was launched in 1993 to provide shoppers with clear and reliable guidance on the environmental quality of a product. The label features stars representing the 15 EU nations in the shape of a flower.

Out of all the people I know, I cannot think of anyone who would not be angry and upset if they saw someone else torturing a defenceless animal. They would do something to try to stop it, like calling a policeman or telephoning the RSPCA, or even interfering themselves.

If people who have respect for animals knew that a certain make of hairspray, for example, had been tested on animals causing them to live in fear and die in pain, I think most of those people wouldn't want to buy it. Buying it would be like turning a blind eye to disgusting behaviour which they would never put up with if they saw it actually happening.

Selling shampoos, hairsprays, detergents, cosmetics, toiletries, etc, without telling people they have been tested on animals seems to be just as dishonest as selling steak pies to vegetarians, telling them only that the pies are very nourishing and tasty.

The EC Ecolabelling Scheme could obviously be useful here because it encourages companies to make products which will not harm the environment. Products which are environmentally friendly can then use the EC logo on their packaging. A perfect solution - except for the boring EC logo, which is a pathetic, weedy-looking thing!

The UK Ecolabelling Board, however, which decides whether products meet their standards to be 'environmentally friendly', seems to think that animals are not part of the environment. It is arguing that a product can be allowed to display the weedy EC logo *even if it has been tested on animals.*

Animals ARE part of the environment! If a product has already destroyed animals' lives in atrocious ways, it has already damaged a part of the environment even before you pour it down the drain.

Products which are NOT included in the EC Ecolabelling Scheme include food, drink and medicines. I suppose that medicines really do have to be left out. If somebody who I loved was ill and they could only be cured with a medicine which was environmentally unfriendly in every way you could think of or they would die, I couldn't just let them die. However, thousands of medical tests on animals are unnecessary, because they have been done so many times before, and you would think that someone would have come up with an alternative to all this cruel waste of lives.

(An alternative I thought of which would really work well is an International Computer Databank, which could be set up to store all the information and results so that companies could just tap into the Database without having to spend a bomb on unnecessary experiments that have been done before.)

It seems to me that the Ecolabelling scheme just isn't living up to its potential. The UK Ecolabelling Board will have to apply some imagination to fertilize their weedy little logo and teach it not to mislead people, or they'll suddenly find no one wants anything to do with them.

Alex certainly isn't alone in this belief, and one organisation in particular – the British Union for the Abolition of Vivisection (BUAV) – has been campaigning *actively* to persuade the UK Ecolabelling Board to change its mind before it's too late.

Dear Alex,

Like you, we find it difficult to understand
why the UK Ecolabelling Board (UKEB) can't see
that it would be wrong to award ecolabels to
products tested on animals. The UKEB tried to
tell us that animal testing wasn't an environmental issue, that it was somehow a separate
'ethical' issue. Like you, we could not accept
this as we believe that respect for all living
creatures must be part of a healthy respect for
our environment. We therefore decided to find
out what the public thought by commissioning an
opinion poll.

Our poll of over a thousand people showed
that 78 per cent of those questioned thought
that animal testing was an important
green/environmental issue, whilst 74 per cent
thought that cosmetics, toiletries and household products that had been tested on animals
should not be eligible for ecolabels.

The young people we questioned (aged 15 to
24 years old) gave an even clearer response - 85
per cent of young people said that they would
not expect products bearing an official European
Union Ecolabel to have been tested on animals.
Although we have taken these results to the UKEB
and the Department of the Environment, they
still haven't changed their view.

I honestly can't tell you why the
Ecolabelling Board won't change its mind. I
suspect it is because the Ecolabelling Board
is made up mainly of representatives from
mainstream industry and because there is no one
on the Board to speak up for the animals who
can't speak for themselves. We asked the UK
Government to appoint someone from an animal
welfare/rights organisation to the Ecolabelling
Board, but they refused.

Extending the scheme to medicines would be
very difficult because almost *all* medicines are
presently tested on animals. We would like to

see all animal tests end because we believe that it is morally wrong to use animals in this way. We also believe that animal tests can be misleading because animal bodies often react to drugs in different ways to our own. For example, morphine which calms people causes marked excitement in cats. And penicillin, one of the human wonder drugs of the 20th century which has saved innumerable lives, is absolutely deadly to guinea pigs and hamsters!

Thankfully, there is now a great deal of research looking at ways of testing medicines without the use of animals. Ideas like your international computer databank could also do a great deal to reduce the numbers of animals which die in these tests. Unfortunately many companies are very poor at sharing the results of research (animal or otherwise) as they believe it is in their commercial interest to keep such results secret once they have paid for them.

Until we have a truly effective Ecolabelling scheme, the best way of making sure that products you buy haven't been tested on animals is to look out for the BUAV's 'Not Tested on Animals' rabbit logo, or to get a copy of our Approved Product Guide _ which lists almost 200 companies which produce 'cruelty-free' cosmetics and household products.

The bottom line is a simple one: if people don't feel they can trust the Scheme, then in the end the Scheme will fail, and I don't believe people will trust the scheme so long as they give awards to animal tested products.

Yours sincerely,

Dr Malcolm Eames
Head of Information and Research

And that's not so very different from the position of the RSPCA – even though these two organisations don't always see eye to eye on animal welfare issues!

Dear Alexandra,

Thank you for your most interesting critique of the EC eco-labelling scheme. You've clearly taken a lot of trouble to obtain information on this issue and I was most interested to read your views.

The aim of the eco-labelling scheme is to help consumers choose the most 'environmentally-friendly' product in terms of its possible effects on river and air pollution, the ozone layer, etc. As you know, there is a wide range of products labelled 'environmentally friendly', and it was felt that most people would appreciate a standardisation of the various product labels on offer. However, as you pointed out, animal testing has *not* been put forward as a criterion for the various product groups. The RSPCA believes that, for an eco-label to have any meaning, animal welfare issues *should* be part of the overall assessment.

That would still leave us with the problem of working out what 'not tested on animals' really means! It might be assumed that a product labelled 'not tested on animals' would mean that no testing whatsoever had been carried out. But this is not necessarily the case. For some companies, it simply means that the *final product* was not tested on animals, even though some of the ingredients in that product may have been tested on animals during the course of production. Other companies use the so-called '5-year' rule, which means a product is labelled 'not tested on animals' provided none of the ingredients has been tested on animals *within the past five years*.

As it happens, the RSPCA believes that the opportunity for reducing animal use and suffering through eco-labelling is probably limited. However, the eco-label *could* provide a useful means of raising public awareness of the extensive use of animals in safety testing of a wide range of products, and highlight the need to speed up the development of humane alternatives to animal testing.

Yours sincerely,
Peter Davies
Director General

Dear Mr Davies,

If I don't answer letters straight away when I get them, then I get in a panic later when I find I haven't answered them because people would think I don't have any manners. The worst thing is trying to think of excuses why I didn't answer sooner! So, thank you very much indeed for going to so much trouble to explain what the RSPCA's position is concerning Ecolabelling and animal testing.

In your letter you say 'the ecolabel could provide a useful means of raising public awareness of the extensive use of animals in safety testing'.

I couldn't agree with you more. One person who has done more than anybody else, in my opinion, for raising awareness of unnecessary animal tests is Anita Roddick. So it *really* upset me when Dad showed me an article in the *Guardian* saying that the RSPCA would be encouraging shoppers to switch from The Body Shop to retailers with 'higher ethical standards', on the grounds that you didn't think their policy went far enough.

I know it would be difficult for somebody like you to admit you were wrong about something, but is this really very clever? There are lots of disgusting people who deserve to be criticised, but Anita Roddick is a good and kind person and doesn't deserve to be criticised in that way.

With best wishes.

Yours sincerely,

Alex Johnston

And we test beers and lagers on these little fellows

Dear Alexandra,

Thank you for your letter following up your previous correspondence with our Director-General. I have been asked to reply on his behalf and I am pleased to have the opportunity to respond to the points you raise.

You express concern in your letter about the RSPCA's attitude to The Body Shop. The article in the *Guardian* was, however, misleading and I enclose a copy of a letter from the RSPCA, clarifying our position which was published in response to that article.

'Your article (RSPCA encourages shoppers to switch from The Body Shop, August 27) is misleading. It implies that the RSPCA is specifically targeting The Body Shop as part of a new campaign. This is most certainly not the case.

The RSPCA is, of course, deeply concerned about the use of animals for testing cosmetics. The public shares its concern and thus the marketing of "cruelty-free" products is a major issue. Various claims are made by cosmetic companies with respect to animal testing. The RSPCA has analysed these and firmly believes that a fixed cut-off date is the most effective in reducing demand for new animal-tested ingredients. In our literature we therefore most actively promote companies committed to this principle, though other companies are listed. This has been so for the last four years. Clearly, this differs from specifically 'encouraging shoppers to switch from The Body Shop' as your headline states.'

Yours sincerely,

Caroline H Vodden (Mrs)
Head of Enquiries Service

Dear Mrs Vodden,

Thank you very much for your letter.

I just *knew* there was something fishy about the article in the *Guardian* and it's nice to know that the RSPCA didn't have anything to do with it. It would have been ridiculous if the RSPCA had picked on somebody like Anita Roddick when there are so many crooks they could have picked on instead. Please tell Mr Davies I will be more careful not to jump to conclusions in future!

It seems wicked that a newspaper can just make up a load of rubbish like that and just publish a few letters saying the article wasn't true instead of apologizing on the front page so everybody can see it wasn't true.

With best wishes.

Yours sincerely,

Alex Johnston

Given such warm support, you won't be surprised to know that Alex also wrote to Anita Roddick herself.

Dear Alex,

Your piece on ecolabelling really touched me. Along with our friends in the animal welfare and environmental organisations we have been battling for nearly two years to make the British and European ecolabelling authorities see sense.

Ordinary people, let alone 'green consumers', just do not draw distinctions between issues like ozone depletion, global warming and animal welfare. You simply *cannot* argue that a product is environmentally OK if its development and manufacture required suffering by animals.

Imagine how cheated someone would feel if they bought a shampoo with an official European Union stamp of ecological approval only to discover when they got home that it had been tested on laboratory animals. It might be enough to put them off being a green consumer for life! Add the EU ecolabel to all the other nonsensical, misleading and misused green claims like ozone friendly, environment friendly, biodegradable, recyclable, etc, and we are heading for a real mess.

The good news is that our friends at the Women's Environmental Network are setting up a consumer help line to assist shoppers who need advice. The WEN Directory of Information (WENDI) can be reached on 0171 704 6800. Also, many pressure groups and retailers are now backing legislation in the British Parliament, which should outlaw misleading green marketing claims forever.

Let us keep our fingers crossed that the campaign groups succeed and that honesty will prevail.

Love and best wishes,

Anita Roddick

Before an ecolabel is awarded, every stage in the products' life is assessed, from the amount of raw materials and energy needed to make it, to the pollution of water, land and air created during its use and after its disposal. Each of these factors is taken into account, and a final 'score' calculated. Products with a sufficiently high score get an ecolabel and those which fail are refused it.

The first EC ecolabels were awarded to three washing machines, in 1993. Other groups of products under study include hairsprays, antiperspirants, light bulbs, kitchen towels, toilet rolls, cleaning products and refrigerators.

Some aspects of the ecolabelling scheme have been criticised. If, instead of the 'pass/fail' system, products were graded (rather like the system of awarding 'stars' to hotels as an indication of quality) consumers would have more information and so be able to make more informed choices about which product is greenest. Another criticism is that participation in the current ecolabelling scheme is voluntary. Companies decide whether or not to submit their products – which means that information is restricted to those limited number of products which are put forward for assessment. And people who make a product that they *know* is harming the environment aren't likely to submit it to the scheme.

So what's going on? Why would an apparently 'green' organisation like the UK Ecolabelling Board deliberately set itself up against organisations like the BUAV and the RSPCA, let alone The Body Shop.

The Chairman of the UK Ecolabelling Board is Dr Elizabeth Nelson, and she found the time to give Alex a very full answer.

Dear Miss Johnston,
Thank you for your letter. I certainly enjoyed reading it.

You have raised a number of very important points, but I think the one that concerns you most is the use of the EU logo on products which might have been tested on animals. Of course animals are part of the environment. But the question here is whether 'tested on animals' should be included as one of the actual 'product criteria' which are used in drawing up the scientific evidence to decide which brands do least damage to the environment.

The things we are looking at include the amount of packaging materials, air pollution, river pollution, energy used, natural resources depleted and destruction of eco-systems. Animal testing is deemed by the majority of European countries *not* to be a relevant criterion for selection of those brands which do least damage to the environment. Animal testing is viewed as an *ethical issue* by the other countries. They make the distinction between animal testing and destruction of species in the natural environment.

As with so many things in the European Union, environmental legislation *must* take into account all of the very different cultures in the Member States.

The compromise which was reached is

that animal testing should be outlawed for cosmetics by January 1998, if suitable alternative testing methods are then available.

The use of animals for testing has fallen dramatically over the last 10 years. You should continue to push for the cessation of animal testing, but I would ask that you consider whether or not we shouldn't press ahead as quickly as possible on a European-wide ecolabelling scheme which *does* take into account many other vital aspects of damage to the environment.

On one or two of your other points. I agree with you that it is a pity that pharmaceutical products, food and drink, are not included in the EU ecolabelling scheme. The reasons given for this are that those markets are subject to an enormous amount of legislation across the Member States already, and that there is already very strict legislation and enforcement regarding the labelling of all three products.

I hope I have answered at least some of your points.

Yours sincerely,

Dr Elizabeth Nelson
Chairman

Alex was very glad to get this answer. She had written to several members of the Ecolabelling Board to get their views, but only Dr Nelson answered. One other member had even rung up to say that it was 'outrageous' to be put under such pressure. (By that stage, she had discovered that it was all in aid of producing a book to encourage children to write letters – which apparently made it all the more outrageous! But why anyone who sits on a public body should not be willing and able to account to a member of the public for their actions is really something of a mystery.)

Dear Dr Nelson,

Thank you very much for your excellent letter
answering my essay about EC Ecolabelling. It was
kind of you to go to so much trouble to explain
your point of view. I really appreciate it.

I can understand 'the distinction between
animal testing and destruction of species in the
natural environment', but I still think it's just
as wrong to torture an animal in a laboratory as
to poison wild creatures in the countryside.
Sometimes you hear about vicious children
torturing cats, etc, and everybody is horrified
that children could do such a thing. I agree that
children like that ought to be punished, but I
can't see how it's any different when adults are
allowed to do it for something as silly as
cosmetics, etc, just because the law says they
can. If something is wrong, then it's *wrong*, and
that's all there is to it.

The law ought to be changed, and if
Ecolabelling Boards in other European countries
are hypocrites, at least we could set a good
example in Britain.

(You said I should 'continue to push for
cessation of animal testing', so that's what I'm
doing!)

It must be a good sign that the number of
animals used for testing has fallen dramatically
over the last 10 years, but I don't think it
should be about numbers. The suffering of one
animal which is being tortured in that way isn't
any the less because it's the only one. If a
politician said 'only one person got tortured
to death in Bosnia today, which is a big
improvement', you would know what he MEANT, but
not many people would vote for that politician

next time there was an election, would they? And it certainly wasn't a 'big improvement' for the person who got tortured to death.

With best wishes.

Yours sincerely,

Alex Johnston

You're a vicious, sadistic monster, Felcombe – Ever thought of a career in a research laboratory?

CAREERS TEACHER

It's all well and good trying to blame such a decision on other European countries (implying that it is their inadequate ethical standards that are at fault), but what Alex was trying to tease out was where ethics ends and political compromise begins.

With that in mind, she had a crack at the Archbishop of Canterbury. Mr Nunn, of the Archbishop's Public Affairs Department replied saying that the Archbishop sympathised with her approach but had many calls on his time and was unable to make an exception in giving his support to this cause. He also pointed out that the Archbishop had demonstrated his concern for *all* animals by becoming the first Vice-Patron of the

RSPCA, and suggested that, in future, Alex kept her letters shorter! This was Alex's reply:

Dear Mr Nunn,

It was very kind of you to give me advice about trying to keep letters short and I know you are right about that, so I will try to make them shorter. It was quite funny when I read your letter to my Dad because he said 'thank you God for sending me an ally'. He would be very happy if my letters were shorter because he types them while I dictate from my draft letter, and he is always asking me to make them shorter.

The reason I wanted to get opinions from different religious leaders was because I think they probably all agree on a lot of things where the environment and animals are concerned. I think people who are cruel to animals probably wouldn't be very kind to people either, so maybe he could write a sermon about how children should be taught to be kind to animals so they will grow up caring about people as well?

It is nice to know that the Archbishop of Canterbury is the first Vice Patron of the RSPCA, because it shows that he cares about *all* God's creatures as well as people. So I am sure he would appreciate the idea of a sermon on this subject.

If he is just too busy, that can't be helped, but could you suggest another Archbishop who I could write to who might have time?

With best wishes.

Yours sincerely,

Alex Johnston

You have to admit that such patience is positively saintly. She didn't even point out to Mr Nunn that he totally failed to answer her specific question about animal testing and ecolabelling! But saintliness was not enough for Mr Nunn, and Alex got a brief two-sentence letter in reply. She tried twice more to get a response from the Archbishop, once again about ecolabelling and once about population. After her second letter (which, to be honest, had completely shifted ground and tried to start up a new theme), Mr Nunn wrote to her again suggesting it was time to close the correspondence and enclosing a press cutting to illustrate his reasons for doing so:

HABGOOD ROUNDS ON LAZY STUDENTS

Students who send begging letters to public figures asking for information are condemned for laziness by the Archbishop of York, Dr John Habgood.

Dr Habgood singles out for criticism requests such as this: 'We are doing God this term. Please send full information and leaflets.'

Dr Habgood says: 'I receive many such letters, not quite so blatantly absurd perhaps, but just as unrealistic about the kind of help it is appropriate to seek. School-children conducting "surveys" and students doing projects send their polite begging letters week after week, asking questions which would take hours to answer properly. My invariable principle is to refer them to published sources; on the principle that it is they who should do their homework, not I.'

While agreeing that writing to public figures out of distress or anger is acceptable, he says surveying public figures as part of one's school or college work is just lazy-mindedness."

[*The Times*, June 2 1993]

This was Alex's reaction:

Dear Dr Carey,

Thank you for asking Mr Andrew Nunn to answer my most recent letter. It is true that Mr Nunn has done his best to be helpful and to let me know that you are a Vice Patron of the RSPCA and I think Mr Nunn is an excellent person.

But I am NOT lazy and I did NOT send you a 'begging letter', which is what Dr Habgood is talking about in his article which you sent me, and which you say you agree with. Dr Habgood's article is full of contempt for students who say

things like, 'We are doing God this term. Please
send full information and leaflets', but most
people would feel sad for anyone who is that
stupid. I do NOT agree that asking you for your
own views on animal experiments and over-
population was stupid in any way at all.

Dr Habgood says: 'My invariable principle is to
refer them to published sources, on the principle
that it is they who should do their homework, not
I'.

The book which I am working on at the moment
may turn out to be one of the 'published sources'
which Dr Habgood mentions. If students could find
the Church of England's views on animal testing
and over-population in my book, maybe they would
stop pestering you and Dr Habgood when they can't
find the answers in the Bible either!

In Dr Habgood's article it says he agrees that
writing to public figures out of distress or anger
'is acceptable'. Well, I wrote my essay out of
distress AND anger, for your information. You will
find the reasons I am less distressed and angry
now in all the wonderful answers I have received
from people who are doing *their* best.

If you think children who ask you for your
opinion about what is right and wrong are
wasting your time, then it would be much better
if you didn't waste poor Mr Nunn's time, let
alone the stamp. Just don't answer! If you do
answer, though, I can't see why it's a problem
to say something worth saying, and say it
yourself.

A Muslim cleric who answered my essay about
animal testing wrote a letter which was only ten
lines long. What he said in ten lines could only
have come from God because it was so beautiful and
it said so much.

Please don't ask Mr Nunn to answer again
because it isn't fair to him, and HE has done *his*
best. I hope you and your family had a lovely
holiday.
      With best wishes.
      Yours sincerely,

           Alex Johnston

The Muslim cleric referred to above was Dr K Alavi of the
Islamic Propagation Centre International.

Dear Miss Alexandra Johnston,
Thank you for your thought provoking letter. I
am sure I have learnt from it. Children are
considered innocent in Islam and therefore
their thoughts are precious. Modern competitive
market economics and the art of advertisement
has created confusion. I agree with you when
you refer to the suffering of an animal used
for such experiments. In the name of scientific
and technological advancement we are causing
damage to the environment and consequently
harming ourselves. I think we should keep up
our pressure so that the people concerned
should keep in mind genuine need and limits for
these experiments.
      Thank you.
      Yours sincerely,
         Dr K Alavi
         For the Islamic Propagation Centre
         International

To be fair to Mr Nunn, that doesn't actually say a great deal
more than Mr Nunn himself had said! But it led to a much
more fruitful exchange.

Dear Dr Alavi,

Thank you for your lovely letter. You've managed to say so much in so few words, which is a much better example for me than what the Archbishop's secretary wrote to me, advising me to write short- er letters!

I'm glad that some people in the world think children's thoughts are precious! Some of the Members of Parliament seem to think that because I'm a child it doesn't matter what my opinion is, and some think that my ideas are not my own, just because Dad types my letters for me to make them easier to read.

Dad says that somewhere in the Holy Koran there is a passage saying that God has given us a herb or a plant to cure every disease. I was thinking about this and it would help to back up another issue I am writing to people about (concerning the preservation of rainforests) if it was true.

     With best wishes.
     Yours sincerely,

          Alex Johnston

Dear Miss Alexandra Johnston,
Thank you for your nice letter and I pray to God Almighty to guide us in understanding the true value of his creation so that we may benefit from it, rather than destroy it.

     With reference to your Dad's idea of a verse in the Qur'an about a herb, I, unfortu- nately, could not find it. There is a lot about trees and gardens as signs of God's work in this world, but no special reference to a herb or tree as a cure for every disease. Qur'an has mentioned the olive tree as a blessed tree and honey as a cure for human disease.

     God is the ultimate source of knowledge.
        Yours sincerely,
         Dr K Alavi

Dear Dr Alavi,

Thank you so much for your charming letter. You must be the first real godly person that I have written to. Dad just laughed when I told him so, but it is true. I have written to Catholic and Anglican clerics but neither of them cares enough about the way people are destroying this planet - well, that's the only thing I can assume from their letters.

When I asked Dad why he never became a Muslim, he said God probably can't see any difference between good Christians and good Muslims. But since he hasn't learnt how to be a good Christian yet, God wouldn't be fooled if he pretended to be a good Muslim instead!

With best wishes.

Yours sincerely,

Alexandra Johnston

Dear Miss Alexandra Johnston,

Thank you for your kind letter. The whole of creation is the family of God, and we should be kind towards each other. I have found a general remark of the Prophet about the medicinal properties of things. He is reported to have said:

'Make use of medical treatment, for God did not cause a disease without assigning a remedy for it, with exception of the disease of old age.'

Yours sincerely,

Dr K Alavi

Dear Dr Alavi,

I am glad you agree that the whole of creation is the family of God. People with different religions ought to respect each other and learn from each other, and not always pretend that only THEY know what God thinks about something. The only Christian clerics who are worth listening to in my opinion are the ones who try to behave like Jesus did, which *you* obviously do even though you are a Muslim, so you must be a good Christian as well.

I expect God just wants people to respect each other and doesn't care at all whether they are one religion or another. It's hard to know how an Indian in the Amazon forest could be a Christian or a Muslim or a Jew if he hadn't even heard of any of them. But he could still be a good person and a part of the family of God. It wouldn't be very fair if he wasn't, would it, especially if he hadn't messed up God's creation the way a lot of Christians and Muslims and Jews have done?

With best wishes.
Yours sincerely,
Alex Johnston

Dear Miss Alexandra Johnston,

Modern man with his technical know-how cannot be considered under-privileged, like primitive people. Modern man is a crook, mischievous and rebellious against God. Having knowledge of some aspects of God's creation, he has assumed that he has absolute authority over God's creation and feels free to play with the creation. According to the Qur'an, this is not a new phenomenon. Many early people on the basis of their civilisation and culture boasted of their power and disobeyed God. What happened to them is a matter of history. Nations, people and civilisations simply disappeared; only names and signs remain (Qur'an 69:1-8; 89:6-14).

I appreciate your honest, balanced and clear views.
Yours sincerely,
Dr K Alavi

'Honest, balanced and clear views' is not a bad commendation. Alex had to call on all her honesty, clarity and balance in addressing herself to the next big campaign – new roads, and cars, and bikes, and the thousands of animals that get squashed on our roads every year.

But first, just in case you've forgotten what this chapter was all about . . .

TIME FOR ACTION!

As Malcolm Eames said in his letter to Alex:

'The bottom line is a simple one: if people don't feel they can trust the Scheme, then in the end the Scheme will fail, and I don't believe people will trust the Scheme so long as they give awards to animal-tested products.'

Astonishingly, this whole matter is still undecided. The UK Ecolabelling Board continues to argue that other European countries simply won't accept the inclusion of animal welfare concerns in the Ecolabelling Scheme.

The campaigners continue to argue that no labels should be awarded for cosmetics without those animals' welfare concerns being taken on board.

So what do *you* think? Are you part of that 85% of young people polled by the BUAV who said they would not expect products bearing an ecolabel to have been tested on animals? Or do you think these are different issues?

This is the time to let Dr Nelson of the UK Ecolabelling Board know what you feel:

Dr Elizabeth Nelson
Chairman
UK Ecolabelling Board
7th Floor, Eastbury House
30-34 Albert Embankment
London SE1 7TL

Chapter 4
GETTING PLACES

Most people really are in two minds about cars. Those who are lucky enough to have one enjoy the freedom it brings, but feel bad about the problems it causes. Traffic jams are always somebody else's fault, not ours!

But whether we love cars or hate them, almost everyone agrees that the pollution and congestion they cause can't go on like this.

More cars on our roads means more pollution, particularly in towns and cities, with more and more people (especially young people) suffering from asthma and other health problems. It also means more damage to the countryside as new roads continue to carve through some of the most beautiful parts of our country. And it means more carbon dioxide pumping out into the atmosphere worsening the problem of global warming.

So why is change so slow to come? Alex set out to quiz some of the politicians who have to wrestle with this dilemma, including ministers past and present, the campaigners who've been giving them such a hard time over the last few years, and a couple of independent experts who would like to think they're one degree removed from the heat of the battle. Here is what she wrote:

There is a road going to just about every place in the whole wide world, and it's obvious that we must have enough of them by now in Britain. If we don't want any more roads, we don't *have* to have them. But it is up to all of us to say 'enough is enough'. It's not fair to just let a few protestors stand in the rain for the rest of us while we don't do anything to help.

Trying to preserve our countryside is not

just important to us - it's really important
for the welfare of future generations who
will have to live on the muck-heap of a planet
that adults have allowed to be created, with
the help of careless businessmen who think
money is the only thing that matters. If
these people are really as intelligent as
they seem to think they are, they should ask
themselves what good money will do for their
children when their children can't breathe!

Some of the ideas ordinary people have had
for slowing down the mad rush for more and
more roads and more and more cars are really
exciting. In spite of getting very little
help from the Government, an organisation
called Sustrans is going from strength to
strength. This organisation goes around
building cycle-paths wherever it can get
permission from local Councils, farmers and
land-owners to do it. Because the cycle-paths
are made with the help of volunteers, it
doesn't cost the earth to build one. To give
an idea of the cost of building a cycle-path
compared with what it costs to build a road:
a National Cycle Route going all the way from
Inverness to Dover would cost less than
widening just two miles of the M25 Motorway!

If the Government would agree, then cycle-
paths could be built alongside existing
roads with trees and plants and hedgerows
separating the two. That way more people
would cycle, especially for short local
journeys, because they would feel safer doing
it and parents would not have to worry about
their children being knocked over and
squished flat by a passing lorry, etc. So why
not? Is it because nobody makes money out of

cycle-paths, and not many people make a lot
of money out of bicycles?

A problem that really upsets me about
country roads is the number of animals that
get knocked down by cars which go too fast.
Especially in the Spring, which is supposed
to be the season of new life, not death, for
a passing rabbit or squirrel. To knock two
problems on the head at the same time, I
think it would be a good idea to have *hollow*
'sleeping policemen' (the bumps on the roads
which stop car drivers from speeding) built
into all country roads, so that animals could
pass through the tunnels and car drivers
would either have to slow down or break their
cars and bash their heads on the roof. An
alternative idea would be to have deep dips in
the road which would do the same thing, narrow
enough for a car's wheels to pass over and
deep enough for animals not to get squished.

I can understand why people get sick of
traffic clogging up the towns where they
live. But if Town Councils were to put up
huge signs before alternative routes which
already go around towns saying 'WARNING:
£5 Council Toll for non-residents of
(wherever)', perhaps there would soon be no
need for a bypass? The Council would be very
happy with all the extra money, I expect.

If children can have sensible ideas (and I
think these ideas are reasonable and wouldn't
be very expensive), I am hoping that you and
some other grown-ups I write to will be able
to think of some useful ideas too - the sort of
things which could actually work and improve
the world we all have to live in. I will put
the best ones in a book which I am writing.
(Fun letters are best, not stuffy ones!)

When Alex first started sending out this letter, the Minister for Roads and Traffic was a man called Robert Key. He'd gone on the record saying how much he loved cars and the wonders of the internal combustion engine, and was so enthusiastic that environmentalists came to know him as Mr Toad!

But when the civil servants at the Department of Transport eventually got round to answering Alex's letter, he was no longer Minister for Roads. That particular job had been abolished – but the roads haven't.

Dear Ms Johnston,
Thank you for your letter of 6 July to Robert Key (who you may know is no longer Minister for Roads and Traffic) about road building and a number of other issues.

Whilst I very much respect your views, it has to be remembered that a good national and local road network is needed to assist economic growth. A very large number of people depend on good roads to transport their goods and for their employment. But I agree there is a need to reduce the environmental impact of road transport.

1. All schemes in the national roads programme *are* subject to environmental assessment. An Environmental Statement is published for all schemes which will have a significant effect on the environment. *Every effort* is made to design roads sensitively to fit into the landscape as closely as possible. In cases where it is impossible to avoid protected areas, the greatest care is taken to reduce the impact by careful design and the use of planting and landscaping techniques. In appropriate situations, plant and animal species may be relocated.
2. You asked specifically about underground crossings for animals. These have been provided in some locations, and if properly located, *can* be successful. I am afraid it is just not possible to provide them on all country roads. In reality, there is very little that can be done to prevent road accidents to small animals in the countryside.
3. You also refer to the idea of charging people to take their car into towns. The Department has a major research project underway to consider this issue. It must be remembered that many businesses, particularly the tourist industry, rely on visitors. Such cities are not likely to favour a tax on visitors!
4. There is certainly scope for an increase in cycling to help reduce pollution and traffic congestion. However, in many instances there is no alternative to car use, and some car journeys would not be practicable to undertake by bicycle. It is also not realistic to compare the work of Sustrans with major road building. Nor is it practical to provide a cycle route alongside every new road, as you suggest.
5. You may also be surprised to learn that the Department of Transport has had a long association with Sustrans, starting with a survey of disused railway lines which Sustrans did for the Department in the early 1980s. We keep in touch with progress on conversion work, and

have recently announced that we will be providing funds to Sustrans to carry out a feasibility study into a proposed cycle route along the line of the Thames between Hampton Court and Dartford.

I hope this letter goes some way to answering the questions you raised and convinces you that you are not alone in caring for the environment. Policies are designed to improve matters *not* make them worse.

Yours sincerely,

R Richards
DITM Division

Dear Mr Richards,

Thank you very much for going to so much trouble to answer my essay and my letter to Robert Key MP. Especially as he's no longer the Minister.

I *know* that I am not alone in caring for the environment, and it's reassuring that there are people like you in the Department of Transport who would seem to care about it as well. The problem seems to be that it is Ministers who make the decisions, and if their decisions are wrong, then the only thing people can do is lie down in front of bulldozers!

From the answers which I have received, I am still convinced that the solution is *not* to build new roads, however carefully they are planned. Much more money ought to be spent on improving public transport instead of on new roads.

I am back at school now, so it is difficult to find the time to answer letters properly, but thank you very much for doing your best to come up with some answers.

With best wishes.
Yours sincerely,

Alex Johnston

There are currently over 26 million motor vehicles in the UK – the vast majority being private cars – and numbers are growing all the time.

Between 1982 and 1992, the number of miles travelled by motor vehicles in the UK rose by some 43 per cent.

The Government's response to traffic growth has been to try to provide for it by building more roads, at a cost of billions of pounds. However, it recently admitted that it recognised this simply led to more traffic.

Many unique national heritage sites and wildlife habitats are threatened by road schemes. Others, such as Twyford Down, one of the most important and protected landscapes in the country, have already disappeared under tarmac.

Alex had also written to another Conservative MP, Sir Geoffrey Pattie, one of a handful of Tory MPs opposing the Government's plans to widen the M25 – which just happens to go through his constituency of Chertsey and Walton! This makes him a very important man, and much more of a worry to the Department of Transport than all the Labour MPs put together. With such a small majority in the House of Commons, the Government can't afford too many rebels on its own side. Alex certainly did her best to get something juicy out of him:

> 'I think you were very brave to say that you thought widening the M25 was a rotten idea, because politicians always get into trouble when they say what they think instead of just going along with what they are told to think, so I would be interested to know your ideas as well, about how to solve some of the problems.'

She was therefore a bit surprised when she heard back not from Sir Geoffrey but from an MP to whom she *hadn't* written.

Dear Alex,

My colleague, Sir Geoffrey Pattie, has passed on your letter to my office at Westminster today regarding the M25 and your concerns for the environment and the countryside.

I am interested to learn about the organisation 'Sustrans'. I would be grateful if you could please let me have some more information about them, and if they are undertaking any work within the Hexham area.

It was fascinating to read your ideas.

Yours sincerely,

Peter Atkinson

Not much about the M25, or about any roads at all come to that. Peter Atkinson is Alex's MP for Hexham, up in Northumberland, and just about as far away from the M25 as you can get! Mr Atkinson's secretary explained why he'd said this later:

> 'There is a strict Parliamentary convention that Members of Parliament only correspond with their own constituents.'

In fact, Sir Geoffrey Pattie soon relented – or his secretary did:

Dear Alexandra,

In the light of your earlier letter, which Sir Geoffrey thought was so good, he thought you would like to have the enclosed copy of Runnymede Council's alternative proposals to the widening of the M25. From this you will see there are several measures which can be taken which improve traffic flow without having to ruin the countryside and destroy wildlife by putting down more concrete.

Sir Geoffrey hopes that you will one day come to the House of Commons to have tea with Peter Atkinson and that he may join you.

Yours sincerely,

B. Campbell (Miss)
Secretary

Dear Sir Geoffrey,

Thank you very much for your letter, with the copy of Runnymede Council's alternative proposals to the widening of the M25. It was very kind of you to send it to me.

I'm glad you decided to pay no attention to the strict convention that Members of Parliament only correspond with their own constituents. It doesn't seem a very sensible convention to me, and I expect some people must get quite upset when they write to someone and get an answer from somebody else who might not even understand what they were talking about. It sounds a bit like the Common Agricultural Policy, if you know what I mean!

I don't often come to London, but I would love to have tea with you and Mr Atkinson if I have to go for a meeting with the publishers or go to London for some other reason. That would be great, and it was very kind of you to suggest it.

Yours sincerely,

Alex Johnston

Motor vehicles are the fastest growing source of air pollution in the UK today. Traffic fumes are a leading cause of smog in cities, towns and rural areas.

Fumes and sooty particles from cars and other motor vehicles can aggravate asthma and other breathing problems. Asthma kills around 2,000 children and adults each year. The number of children admitted to hospital for asthma more than doubled between 1976 and 1992.

Over 4000 people are killed and 300,000 injured on our roads every year.

It's never easy getting information out of MPs, whichever party they happen to belong to. But one MP came up trumps. Peter Bottomley, Conservative MP for Eltham, is himself a very keen cyclist and was once a Minister in the Department of Transport. So he should know what he is talking about! He is now one of those backbench MPs with a well-earned reputation for saying what he thinks.

Dear Alexandra,
I have, today, seen your letter. Before getting to the important areas of agreement between us, you should be aware of the fact that very little of our countryside is given over to roads. And those roads are built only if they are *necessary,* not just because they are desired. They often have *good* consequences:

- Changing economic geography, allowing people to work and go on living in areas such as Northern Ireland, Scotland and the North of England, Wales and the South West.
- Environmental improvement, such as the A2 Rochester Way relief road in my London constituency or certain bypasses.
- Casualty reduction, separating vulnerable road users on two feet or two wheels from people speeding through in their warm protected steel cars, listening to the wireless programmes instead of caring for you or me trying to cross the local road in the rain in safety.

Some people appear to think that car driving was all right when motorists were male, white, middle-aged, middle class and in full time work. Now, many women, retired people, young people, poor people, and ethnic minorities drive and own cars. I am not impressed by the idea that a change should be introduced with the intention of restricting the use of the motorcar to people with a fistful of five pound notes - ie. mainly male, white, middle class, etc . . . !

I *do* believe we should develop public transport to attract people who have a real choice, rather than, say, leaving buses to be used by people who don't have any choice.

I *do* believe in changing the culture, so those like me who can change their place of work or their home try to halve the time to and from work. That has all kinds of advantages.

And I *do* believe that a fixed proportion of transport spending should go on the most used method - walking. If half of one per cent of rail and road money was used for cycling and walking, there could be many winners.

I look forward to being able to give up driving. You have probably been looking forward to me ending this letter!

      Yours sincerely,

          Peter Bottomley

Dear Mr Bottomley,
Thank you very much for your excellent letter,
answering my letter and my essay about road-build-
ing in Britain. It was a bit hard to read your
handwriting so Dad read it aloud to me and it was
really interesting. I think it is the best letter
I have received from a politician. Not that
there's that much competition at the moment.

Yesterday I received a good letter from a
journalist saying that he can do four extra hours
of work in one day by travelling on a train instead
of driving. He uses a lap-top computer and a mobile
telephone. Driving to work in traffic jams seems
like a real waste of time, but the trouble with
going on the train is it's so expensive.

And isn't it true that the Government gets so
much money from taxes like road tax and petrol
that it doesn't really want anybody to stop using
the roads, even if everybody is getting choked by
the fumes?

With best wishes.
Yours sincerely,

Alex Johnston

Around this time the Royal Commission on Environmental Pollution produced a very hard-hitting report on transport issues. Its main recommendations were that the price of petrol should be doubled and spending on the road programme halved – suggestions which have not been well-received by the Department of Transport, but which had Alex dancing around in delight at the idea of such a serious and ever so eminent group of people coming up with such 'good ideas'! By which I think she meant *her* ideas.

As well as the officials, Alex wrote to two independent experts, the first being Dr John Whitelegg, who replied almost by return of post just to prove that some people really have got their correspondence pile under control!

Dear Alex,

Thank you very much indeed for writing to me, and let me say how much I appreciate the trouble you have taken to put your thoughts down onto paper and get them to me.

The first thing I would like to say is that I could not agree more with your general approach. There is no doubt in my mind that continuing to build roads, and therefore to encourage higher and higher levels of traffic, is an extremely serious mistake which we will (if we are lucky!) live to regret. Building roads simply encourages higher levels of traffic and encourages people to drive longer distances to carry out very basic everyday tasks that they would be much happier and healthier doing by bike, by foot or by public transport.

New roads, particularly bypasses around towns and cities, take up a great deal of valuable land and do a great deal of damage in terms of dead wildlife and poor air quality. They also encourage higher levels of car and lorry use, and therefore in their turn create the demand for more new roads in the future, making the whole process more and more difficult to resolve when we finally get round to resolving it!

All these problems have local, regional, national and global consequences. It is quite clear that, *globally*, we're in for a lot of trouble from greenhouse gases, particularly carbon dioxide from transport. We currently have 500 million vehicles globally, and this could well rise to 2.5 billion when Eastern Europe, the former Soviet Union, China, India, etc, acquire the vehicles that they think are the mark of modernisation and progress − because they have learnt that from us.

I am convinced that children do have very sensible ideas and I would like to encourage you to continue working and writing in this way, and to write to your own local council, your MP and to the Secretary of State for Transport. And why not the Prime Minister while you're about it?

I think it would be of very real value if a number of children of your age could band together and put forward a clear manifesto for the future. I don't see any reason at all why you should sit back and allow people aged between 40 and 60, usually male, driving round in cars, to plan the future that they will not experience because they will be dead. They are currently designing the future that *you* will have to live in, and *your* views should play a more prominent part in that design process.

I wish you the very best of luck. I really did enjoy your letter, and even though these are very serious issues, I would encourage you to retain that sense of humour!

Yours sincerely,

John Whitelegg

Dear Dr Whitelegg,

I was very pleased to receive your letter in the post this morning, answering mine, and it was very kind of you to take so much trouble to write such a brilliant letter.

Your idea of a number of children of my age banding together and putting forward 'a clear manifesto for the future' is an exciting one. At the moment I am concentrating on writing letters for this book, and I am hoping that lots of other children might want to get involved when they read the book and see that it is worth writing to adults like you to find solutions to the problems which worry them. So I think your idea would be a good next step.

With kindest regards.

Yours sincerely,

Alex Johnston

There are less damaging ways of moving people around! Walking and cycling do virtually no damage to the environment and are good exercise as well.

Oxford has been promoting alternatives to car use since the early 1970s. Since then cycling has increased by 12 per cent and city centre car use has remained level.

Buses and trams can be ideal for short trips and commuting. In some cities, like Manchester and Sheffield, trams and light railways are being successfully reintroduced.

The other independent expert Alex wrote to was Dr John Adams, who for years has been pointing out the absurdity of current transport policies. Somehow he manages to do it in a way that gets both civil servants and politicians hopping with rage!

Dear Alex,
Thank you for your splendid letter.

First, a jokey idea; fit all cars with long, sharp spikes emerging from the centre of their steering wheel! Motorists would then drive less, and more slowly and more carefully.

Secondly, why can't we think about the possibility of establishing 'street fleets'? The average car spends about 95 per cent of its life parked. Reserved parking would be made available for a mixed fleet of vehicles for hire (from minis to minibuses). They would be super-vised by a resident fleet co-ordinator and would be available to 'club' members. With the help of computers, smart cards and on-board meters, access could be made quick and convenient. Drivers would be charged on a time/mileage basis. You could then reduce parking spaces for non-fleet cars, increasing the street space devoted to pedestrians, cyclists, children and vegetation. The job of co-ordinator would be particularly suitable for someone living in the street seeking a local job.

Good luck with your book.
Yours sincerely,

John Adams

Dear Dr Adams,

Thank you so much for going to the trouble of writing to me. Excellent ideas - far better than some of mine! The most brilliant idea, I thought, was about hiring cars from a club only when you need one, and only when you're a member. And it would reduce unemployment as well.

There was one passage I didn't think much of, when you say 'increasing the street space devoted to PEDESTRIANS, cyclists, CHILDREN, and vegetation'. Why have you put pedestrians and children separately? Can't WE be pedestrians TOO? Or do we have to be second-class citizens? UNLESS, of course, you meant playgrounds, in which case that's OK!

The idea about spikes being stuck in the middle of the steering-wheels was very funny and made me think. Drivers would probably end up driving from the passenger seat, or sitting on the floor with a periscope, increasing the gamble but avoiding the risk of being skewered!

Thanks again for your letter and articles.
With kindest regards,

Alex Johnston

In York, a large central area of the city has been pedestrianised, and special routes designed for bikes and buses. Walking and cycling have increased, and car use across city centre bridges is only 2 per cent greater than it was in 1965.

For long-distance travel and freight, trains are more efficient and produce less pollution than cars or lorries.

In order to transport one passenger one kilometre, a full car uses over four times as much energy as a full suburban electric train.

TIME FOR ACTION!

No one is arguing that we should get rid of all cars tomorrow! For many people the car is a necessity, especially in rural areas.

For those who do have a car, the first step is to distinguish between *necessary uses* and *unnecessary uses*.

So why don't you keep a log of what the family car is being used for? Just jot down in an old exercise book the date, the reason why the car is being used, and the mileage. This is where you have to be something of a mathematician! You will need to know how many miles to the litre the car does. On a monthly basis, you can then calculate the mileage that could have been avoided if the car hadn't been used for all those unnecessary purposes.

Then calculate how many litres of fuel have been saved. If it is petrol the car is using, multiply that figure by 2.4 (or if it is diesel, by 2.7) to give the *total kilograms of carbon dioxide* (CO_2) that could have been prevented from drifting up into the atmosphere, adding to the problems of global warming.

You will be surprised how much all this can stack up. A typical car user is responsible for the emission of around 3.7 tonnes of carbon dioxide pollution every year – the average car produces 4 times its own weight of carbon dioxide every year.

If you are into calculations of this sort, the Friends of the Earth booklet called *Take the Heat off the Planet* (price £3.45, from FoE Publications, 56-58 Alma Street, Luton, Beds LU1 2YZ) is full of handy tips for saving energy and then working out all the benefits that you can achieve in the process.

On to the next challenge – perhaps the biggest challenge of them all: population!

Chapter 5
POPULATION PROVOCATION!

It took until roughly 1800 for the human population to reach the first billion (that's 1000,000,000). The second billion was reached in 1928 – only 128 years after the first. The third human billion was reached only 32 years after that, in 1960, and the fourth billion was added in only 14 years. The fifth, in 1987, took a mere 13 years, and we are now well on the way to six billion.

This kind of population growth is a problem both in the industrial world (with more people using more energy and resources, causing more pollution and waste) and in the Third World where the impact can be much more immediate: growing food shortages, water shortages, soil erosion, disappearing forests and so on.

Population is just about the most controversial issue that anyone interested in the environment has to deal with. Everyone has their own ideas about it, and it is sometimes quite hard getting the real facts across in the midst of such intense feelings and firmly held opinions!

Alex was putting her ideas together in the run-up to the United Nations Conference on Population and Development which took place in Cairo in September 1994.

This wasn't just another UN Conference; it was the occasion when ideas about how to deal with an overcrowded world were all brought together in a new Action Plan.

The Conference got a lot of coverage in the press, largely because of the row over abortion and other disputes between the Vatican and the rest of the delegates. Unfortunately, the actual *outcome* of the Conference got a lot less coverage, despite the fact that agreement was reached on by far the best Action Plan the United Nations has ever come up with.

But first, here's her letter:

Watching the news on TV is enough to kill off anyone's happy spirit because it is *so* depressing. One thing you can be sure of is that there will ALWAYS be close-up pictures of the victims of famine, drought, war and disease. So it isn't surprising that people who watch the news get what Bob Geldof called 'compassion fatigue'. I think what he meant by this was that because there are so many disasters in our over-crowded world, people will just think to themselves, 'Oh well, ALL that misery is just too much for me to cope with - so why bother to do anything at all if it's just going to be like a drop in the ocean?'

Many people sitting watching TV might just think that these disasters are ways of reducing population and they can't be helped.

Well, they CAN be helped, and you only have to imagine that one of the victims on television is somebody you know if you ever start thinking like that. Then you would start wishing that you could at least do something to help that ONE person even if you couldn't help millions of people all at the same time.

An obvious way to reduce over-population in developing countries is to persuade people to have fewer children, But that doesn't work. In farming areas, especially, it doesn't work for one very bad reason. Having dozens of children is like an old-age pension and a cheap work-force all rolled into one because as long as the children survive they can help herd cattle and goats, dig in the fields and so on. And if any of them survive long enough to get a job, they are expected to look after their pesky parents when they are old.

You only have to see which adults in Kenya (teachers, doctors, company directors, scientists) for example, have two or three children and look after them properly to realise what the solution must be - EDUCATION!

Of course, you can't teach an old dog new tricks, and some fathers are too stuck in their ways to change. So the ones you have to concentrate on are the next generation - the children. The kids of Kenya are desperate for education, probably because they don't want to grow up stupid like their dads who say that everything which is their own fault is just 'Shauri ya Mungu', which means 'God's Law'.

When I was a tiny tot of four I went to a village school near Mombasa in Kenya, where all the children except me were Africans. I was lucky because I had lots of books at home. Most of the other children didn't even have ONE book, but ALL of them could still read and write by the time they were six just from learning at school. In fact, not even the teacher had books, so she wrote stories and alphabets on pieces of paper at home and brought them to school. (I have forgotten most of my Swahili now, but still remember some of the songs we had to learn to sing.)

Books in Kenya are really expensive, so it would be wonderful if schoolchildren in Britain could 'twin' their schools with village schools around the Third World and send them textbooks, which needn't even be new. Children who enjoy writing letters could make pen-pals, which would be really interesting. And it wouldn't only help the education of those in Third World countries, but children in Britain could learn an awful lot as well.

In the case of Kenya, parents who wanted to get involved could send books to 'Maendeleo ya Wanawake', which is like a Women's Institute and means 'women on the move' in Swahili. In Kenya, women have to do most of the work, so uneducated women are much more keen to improve their way of life than the lazy men are. When women learn about the advantages of birth-control, they are much more likely to do something about it because they are the ones who suffer the most from producing too many children, while the men just sit in the sun saying, 'Oh dear, another of my little workers has bitten the dust. Shauri ya Mungu. Mary will just have to work a bit harder'.

I would not want to insult Catholics, but I do think the Pope is a bit like an African man who sits under a mango tree saying, 'Shauri ya Mungu'.

It MUST be wrong for people who don't WANT any more children to go on having them, but the Pope tells Catholics that they shouldn't use artificial methods of birth-control because that wouldn't be God's law - ie. it wouldn't be 'Shauri ya Mungu' any more! Surely if there is something God DOES want, it must be happy, contented children and not millions of skinny kids dying like flies because there is not enough love and food to go around? I think that God might have something to say to the Pope about putting words into God's mouth.

Once people have been educated and can understand the advantages of birth-control it is a terrible thing to put more obstacles in their way, making them feel guilty by saying, 'God doesn't want birth-control'.

It would be more valuable, in my opinion,

for ONE family in Britain to send ONE textbook
to ONE child in ONE Third World country than
for the British Government to give a million
pounds in Development Aid to the Government in
that country, much of which somehow gets
slipped into the pockets of far too many of
their so-called politicians. At least a book
cannot do any harm, and future generations
don't have to scrape and save to pay it back.

If EVERY British family sent one book to
one child, it would be like the saying, 'look
after the pennies and the pounds will look
after themselves', and perhaps we would not
have to suffer from 'compassion fatigue'
EVERY time we switch on the television. Maybe
we could imagine that an African doctor is
someone we know and it was US who sent him,
or her, their first book! Think how many
people a doctor could be helping from our
'drop in the ocean'!

The first person Alex sent her letter off to was Norman Myers. Of all the 'world experts' on this subject, Dr Myers has written and spoken more knowledgeably, more eloquently and more often than almost anyone else in the business. He also knows the importance of treating people's ideas with respect – even if they are only 13 years old.

Dear Alex (if I may),
What a splendid surprise to see your letter. Thanks so much for writing to me, and telling me about all your thoughts and feelings in such a vivid fashion. I admire your awareness and convictions, and I want to write back to you straight away.

It is precisely letters like yours that give me extra hope that we can still save our 'Only One World'. Frankly, reading your letter made me feel that there is a lot still to play for. I shall keep your letter in a file that contains just a few special pieces that I have collected over the past decades, and from time to time I shall get it out and re-read it whenever I need a 'boost'.

I think the main thing is not to lose heart. Or rather to keep looking out for the positive sides. I remain firmly convinced, despite stacks of downside news, that we can still turn profound problems into glorious opportunities. There are so many things that we can still do to save a dismal situation; and it certainly need not cost us the Earth to save the Earth. On the contrary, a lot of the things we can do to help the environment will help the economy too, so we shall come out ahead on more than one front.

You speak about writing letters, in conjunction with your friends at school. Yes!, there is much advantage in this. It may not sound so glamorous as sitting in front of bulldozers, but I think that in the long run it can be just as productive. Why not send periodic letters, perhaps once a month, on some environmental or conservation issue - trees, litter, recycling, whatever - to your MP, with a copy to John Major and to your local newspaper, preferably signed by as many of your schoolfriends as you can persuade to add their signatures?

Did you know that MPs reckon that for every one letter they receive, there are another twenty letters 'out there' that do not get written but would certainly arrive on MPs desks if the potential writers believed it was worth their time? In any case, MPs regard letters from children as letters from people who are going to be voting for a longer period into the future than is the case with adults!

But saving our world is a great act of faith anyway. Remember that with modern communications, you live at a time when nobody need be nobody and everybody can be somebody. You clearly have some very strong opinions: let other people know how you feel. Send copies of your letters to other organisations, such as your local radio station: who knows, you may be invited to a radio studio to say a few words, and I can tell from your letter that you could put over some pretty forceful views in just a few minutes. Go for it!

I am struck by your comments on Kenya. I spent twenty-four very happy years there. When I returned to Nairobi for a conference a little while ago, I took along a complete bag of books to distribute to local schools. You are absolutely bang on target when you suggest that if, say, every tenth person in Britain were to send just one book once a year, that would make a huge heck of a difference.

I am just about to leave for the International Conference on Population and Development in Cairo, and your powerful opinions will certainly go along in my luggage and help me to get further fired up when I speak to leaders from around the world.

I mean that: your letter will have served a thoroughly solid purpose by the time you read this reply.

Thanks again, Alex, for being in touch. Keep your tail up. Again, I admire your spirit, and I am sure you have the wherewithal for keeping on keeping on going in our great battle to save the planet at a time of threat without rival.

Kaa mzima, na nenda salaam.

Norman Myers

Dear Dr Myers,

Thank you very much for your lovely letter! It was kind of you to be so encouraging about my letter and my essay, and it's exciting to think that you will speak up for children at the Cairo conference which you are attending and that my letter might be helpful.

I'm not very keen on writing to politicians any more and if you saw some of the rubbish I have got from them you would see why. One of them rang me up when I was in the middle of writing this letter just now and gave me a lecture about how I was patronising people in the Third World, and he started getting angry. I told him that if I was dying on a dung-heap I would hope somebody would try to help me as well, and all I was doing was trying to help, but he only seemed to be interested in giving me a rocket. Politicians are weird.

Kaa mzima, na nenda salaam. (Keep well and go in peace) I hope everything went well at the Cairo Conference. I have been watching it on TV and looking out for you but so far I haven't seen you.

Yours sincerely,

Alex Johnston

There may already be as many as ten million environmental refugees in the world driven away from their homes and livelihoods as land is lost through soil erosion, desertification and climate change. Bangladesh alone could have 15 million displaced people given a sea level rise of just 0.13 metres as a consequence of global warming.

Food production per person fell in no less than 73 out of 113 developing countries between 1979 and 1991. Of these countries 36 were in Africa. Most countries import the food they cannot produce at home, but not all countries can afford sufficient imports. Over the 1980s, food consumption per person fell in 37 out of 103 developing countries.

To make sure the answers were properly balanced, Alex also wrote to Robert Whelan, the Director of an organisation called the Committee on Population and the Economy. His views are totally opposed to those of Norman Myers, as Alex discovered on reading through the briefing pack he sent her by way of reply. He believes there is no simple relationship between population and damage to the environment, that concern for the environment is often unscientific and more to do with politics than anything else, that the wealth of a country is not hindered by population growth, that food production will always stay ahead of increases in human numbers, and that there is nothing to worry about as regards population! In other words, in his opinion, the United Nations Population Fund and the vast majority of population experts the world over are quite simply off their trolleys and should quietly shut up shop and let people get on with having as many children as they want.

His communication skills are also the very opposite of those of Norman Myers. A scribbled note merely stated: 'I hope you find the enclosed briefing helpful. Like the Archbishop of Canterbury, I don't have time for correspondence!' (Alex had told him about her brush-off from the Archbishop!)

111

Dear Mr Whelan,

Thank you very much for sending me your Population
Information Pack. It is very interesting to read a
different point of view about over population, but
your Information Pack doesn't really answer what I
said in my essay because I couldn't find anything in
it about unwanted, starving children trying to
look after each other on rubbish dumps. I still
think that each one of those children is the most
important part of the whole problem. Maybe irresponsible adults would agree that producing
unwanted children isn't a problem, but I think that
most children would disagree.

It is easy for a man who plants a seed to think
the tree belongs to him, but what about the
gardener who has to look after it? What if the
gardener doesn't want to look after another tree?
I can't see why men shouldn't have a point of view
about it, but if you were a woman and not a man
you might think that women should be the ones who
decide in the end how many children they want to
look after, not the Pope or the Committee on
Population and the Economy! Not even women's
husbands!

Paul Boateng the Labour MP said in a letter
answering my essay: 'A woman has the right to
order her own fertility based on the best possible
clinical advice, information and support'. And I
think he is right. It hasn't got anything to do
with The World Bank, or the Pope or you - just a
woman's right to order her own fertility based on
the best possible clinical advice, information and
support! Information means education, which is
what I said in my essay, and so does clinical
advice. Support means laws which stop men from
interfering!

In your note you said 'Like the Archbishop of
Canterbury, I don't have time for correspondence!',
which I thought was a bit abrupt.

In fact, when I wrote to him on another subject the Archbishop of Canterbury had time to tell somebody else what to write in a long correspondence. Except for saying that I am a lazy girl and I should do my own homework instead of asking important people for their opinions, my essays are too long, etc, he just couldn't think of anything worth saying!

Maybe Mr Boateng should be the Archbishop of Canterbury instead!

With best wishes,

Yours sincerely,

Alex Johnston

Paul Boateng's reply had *really* impressed Alex – partly because she had wound him up something rotten in the letter she wrote him when sending him a copy of her essay on population! (She had suggested that he too was a bit like Robert Whelan, and didn't really care about population, being 'an outspoken defender of people being allowed to have as many children as they want'.) And partly because he came back with such a strong and straight response.

Dear Ms Johnston,

Thank you for your letter which I read with interest.

I suppose as a Politician, I ought to be used by now to being misquoted. I find, however, that I am still capable of getting angry when what I have said is misinterpreted. I have never said that 'over-population is an excellent thing', nor have I ever said anything (whether in the 'outspoken defence of people being allowed to have as many children as they want' or otherwise) that would justify such an interpretation.

I *am* interested, however, in the downright racist criteria that are often applied in defining over-population. When children were being sent down the mines and people were dying of starvation and cold on the streets in nineteenth century Britain, was Britain over-populated? I think not. There was a grotesque imbalance of resources between rich and poor in this country. That remains the case still on a worldwide basis, and the cause remains the same: the unfair allocation of resources between North and South.

I therefore make no apology for saying that *all* people, wherever they live, ought to be allowed to determine for themselves how many children they have. A woman has the right to order her own fertility based on the best possible clinical advice, information and support.

I deeply resent the patronising and high-handed way in which so many in the northern hemisphere believe they have the right to dictate to people living in the south what their pattern of family life should be. This is particularly inappropriate when one considers what a mess so many in the north have made of their own families and communities.

I am also particularly suspicious of the notion that the economic ills of this world can be solved by strictly enforced population control! Rubbish! Quite apart from the question of civil liberties, this ignores the role of the extended family in sustaining communities in so much of the developing world. It also ignores the impact that the wasteful consumption and unfair trading practices of our *own* societies has on the underdevelopment of others.

I hope to live to see a world in which people are able to make informed choices about the number of children they desire, free from the dictates of economic necessity, misguided do-gooders or religion.

Children are the sources (as well as the natural consequences) of so much shared love and joy, that we should work to build a world fit for as many as are born into it.

The issue is one of justice, not numbers.
Best wishes.
Yours sincerely,

Paul Boateng MP

As populations grow, more and more countries will face water scarcity. In 1982, only six African countries with a total of 65 million people faced water shortages. Experts predict that by the year 2000 water shortages will affect 11 countries (with a population of 250 million) and by 2025, 21 countries (with 1.1 billion people) will be affected.

Africa's annual population growth rate of 2.9 per cent makes it the fastest growing region in the world. Asia and Latin America have grown at around 1.8 per cent per year, North America at about 1.1 per cent, the former Soviet Union at 0.5 per cent, and Europe is lowest with 0.3 per cent.

Dear Mr Boateng,

Your letter arrived in the post this morning and it is the FIRST sensible letter I have received from a politician, so getting it was quite an exciting breakthrough! It's lovely to think that there ARE politicians who don't just think 'children should be seen and not heard', which is what most of them seem to think, and it was kind of you to go to so much trouble to let me know your views on this issue. Thank you very much.

I am sorry if the comments which I put in my letter upset you. They were really just meant to be a bit of a tease! Most politicians don't bother to answer at all when they know I am a child, so I have to try to think of ways to provoke them into answering. But I can see you are not like that and you would have answered anyway because you care a lot about it and you have thought about this issue. But I really think you got me wrong. I'm NOT high-handed in any way. I am simply proposing that children in the Third World who will be parents in the future should be educated.

I agree with you that 'downright racist criteria are often applied in defining over-population'. A lot of people don't seem to realise that when an African man or woman dies there is no social security to look after their families, so it is an even bigger disaster for a *lot* of people than if an adult dies in Britain. So it isn't LESS important, it's MORE important! If it wasn't for the extended families which you mention, the families of victims wouldn't have a chance.

I don't know what the solution to racism is because I don't really understand why people think like that. The African teachers at the school which I went to in Kenya obviously thought I was something special because they were much nicer to me than the other children, just because I was

116

white. In a way, the only thing I could complain about was that everybody was a bit *too* kind to me. I know that's not a very reasonable thing to complain about, but it was the way I felt.

When I read about the way some black children get treated in Britain, I feel angry. Children who are different need MORE kindness, not less, because it isn't very nice being different. Maybe fear and ignorance are the reasons for racism, but I couldn't say Africans were afraid or ignorant about me when I was the one who was different. Maybe black people are just nicer than white people, except when they are not always so nice to each other. As I said, I really don't know what the solution is. Maybe there isn't one.

With best wishes,
Yours sincerely,

Alex Johnston

Young people today might very well be curious about the future, wondering what the world's population will be in 2050. The United Nations Population Fund has set an upper and a lower limit, depending on how successful we are in extending access to family planning around the world. The lower limit is a manageable 7.8 billion. The upper limit is a nightmarish 12.5 billion. It's worth comparing the difference between those two figures (4.7 billion) with today's total population figure of 5.7 billion. It is somewhat surprising that the attention of more politicians is not directed at the gap between the two – for it's that gap which will determine the future and the quality of life of all young people today.

At this stage, Alex had reckoned the political debate was just warming up. She was particularly looking forward to a reply from Lynda Chalker, the Government Minister responsible for aid and population matters within the Foreign Office. She'd heard that Lady Chalker had even raised these matters with the Pope himself, so in her letter to Lynda Chalker she said:

'I would love to know what the Pope said when you lectured him, but I don't expect you would tell me that! The best thing he could do is ask children what they think about it. It wouldn't matter if they were rich children or poor children, because they would all tell him the same thing! Anyway, I have said in my essay exactly what *I* would tell him if he asked me, and I'm sorry if it's a bit rude, but it's what I feel.'

The reply was not helpful.

Dear Alexandra,

Baroness Chalker has asked me to thank you for your letter of August 28 about population growth in the Third World. I have been asked to reply.

We read your letter with interest. I attach a recently produced booklet which explains our policies on the provision of overseas aid for population and reproductive health which I hope you will find useful. You may also be interested to read a speech made by Baroness Chalker on July 11 (Population Day).

Yours sincerely,

C A Graham
Health and Population Division
Overseas Development Administration

I wonder if civil servants or Ministers ever understand the depressing effect they can have on young people when they put the lid on such enthusiasm in that way?

Fortunately, Alex fared rather better with Richard Ottaway, Conservative MP, who chairs the House of Commons Parliamentary Committee on Population and Development, and was literally on his way out to the Cairo Conference when he got Alex's letter.

Dear Miss Johnston,

We all know how serious population growth can be and that it is the root cause of many of the world's problems. For example, the tragedy in Rwanda is primarily a territorial dispute brought about by overcrowding. In a recent article in *Atlantic Monthly*, entitled 'The Coming Anarchy', Robert D Kaplan shows how scarcity, crime, overpopulation, tribalism and disease are rapidly destroying the social fabric of our planet, with particular emphasis on Africa. All that is seen in Rwanda, which I believe will be the first of many similar disputes.

It is now widely accepted that people are both the victims and the cause of environmental degradation of the planet. The conference will attempt to come to terms with the realisation that the process of sustainable development is made much more difficult, if not impossible, by the high rates of population growth which prevail when family planning services are not widely available and accepted.

As far as abortion and the Catholic Church are concerned, anyone who studies the subject for more than a few minutes will realise that family planning and abortion are separate matters, and that abortion is the most ineffective and inefficient form of family planning that there could be. No one in their right mind could concede that it is a central part of any family planning programme. I regret that the one person who does not seem to have changed his mind is the Pope and his advisers in the Vatican.

Yours sincerely,

Richard Ottaway

Dear Mr Ottaway,

Thank you very much for your letter. When I wrote my essay about overpopulation I hadn't really discovered very much about the Cairo Conference, so it's interesting to see on TV that a lot of people seem to agree and have the same views as me.

Needless to say the Pope hasn't answered my letter and neither has Cardinal Hume! I don't expect they will, either, but they ought to know what children think about it.

Thank you very much for taking the trouble to write to me.

With best wishes,

Yours sincerely,

Alex Johnston

This is not just a disaster story. In one country after another, average fertility has been falling dramatically over the last 20 years – and in ways that are not necessarily dependent on increases in wealth. The average number of children that a woman in a developing country bears today has dropped from 6.1 in 1965 to just 3.7. In some parts of East Asia, fertility has fallen to near Western levels, which are now below the replacement level of 2.1 per cent in many countries. But in other parts of the world, particularly Africa, reductions in average fertility are happening much too slowly. And a very large number of women (at least 120 million) are denied access to any kind of family planning even though they are *actively* seeking it. That's why we have to take action urgently, today: it will be too late tomorrow.

Dear Miss Johnston,
I am pleased to report that the Cairo
Conference was a great success. We now have
in place a global action plan in which all
countries of the world have addressed the
problem of overpopulation and have come up with
a proposal for dealing with it.

The most significant development is the
recognition that empowerment of women has a
vital role to play in this. I met a female
Nigerian delegate at the conference who told me
she has 6 children. Her aim was to ensure that
she did not have 36 grandchildren! We need
women to be educated and respected, then they
will be liable to have less children. We want
contraception to be available on demand around
the globe. If all this can be achieved then
we really will be on the way to a better
environment for you and your children when you
grow up.

Yours sincerely,

Richard Ottaway

Dear Mr Ottaway,

Judging from some of the letters I have received
on this issue, some people are suspicious that it
isn't just unwanted children Western policy-makers
are worried about. Some people think Western
policy-makers want to keep the Third World over-
populated for selfish reasons. I don't know if
that is true or not, but in my opinion unwanted
children are the most important problem.

With best wishes,
Yours sincerely,

Alex Johnston

As it happens, I really *don't* think it is for selfish reasons that people in countries like this worry about population problems in countries like Kenya. But it is true that we shouldn't worry about them in isolation, and it's also true that justice and the elimination of poverty are just as important — as is argued very powerfully by all the big development charities here in the UK. Alex was delighted to hear back from Vicky Johnson of Action Aid.

Dear Alex,
Thanks for your letter.

Action Aid believes that 'Global Gloom-Mongering', as we put it, is unhelpful. Talking about over-population and environmental devastation or destruction is dramatic, but practical solutions lie in listening to men, women, girls and boys on the ground.

Far from having to persuade people to have fewer children, as you say in your letter, there are many women with whom we work already asking for the means to limit their family size and have fewer children. The World Health Organisation (WHO) estimates that at least 120 million women in developing countries would like to plan their families, but do not have the access to family planning services. Every effort must be made to ensure that these people are provided with the means to limit their family size if they so wish. We also need to address their poverty so that they are in a position to make real choices.

I don't think it is right for you to call the men stupid. With that starting point, we would never get anywhere with population projects. Women's needs have to be central to the population programmes, but we have to understand the different perspectives of *all* the members of the family. Parents will not easily break traditions and customs built up over many years. They may well continue to send their sons to school and not their daughters, and continue to have children until they get enough sons unless parents are also educated. Education for girls has been shown to be one of the

most powerful ways of reducing family size throughout the world.

I do very much agree with you that linking
schools and people is a good idea, especially as we
have so much to learn from people in different
parts of the world. After all, however poor people
in such countries are, and however hard they work,
you still see more people looking happy there than
you do on the London Underground!

I can go round the corner to the doctor and I can
decide when I want to have children. I would like
women everywhere to be able to do the same. I think
that the way to do this is to help individuals and
communities to take charge of their *own* development,
and one of the best ways of doing this is to help
support the various charities here in the UK.

We all need to keep open minds and be willing to
learn from other people because we do *not* always
know best! I am glad you are challenging people,
and that you say we should ask what children in
developing countries think about it themselves.

Yours sincerely,

Vicky Johnson

In the 1950s, Asia accounted for 55 per cent of the world's
population, Europe for 16 per cent and Africa for 9 per cent.
By 1993, Asia accounted for 60 per cent, while Africa had
already replaced Europe in second place. By the year 2015,
Africa is expected to have 19 per cent of the world's population, and Europe just 6 per cent.

In many developing countries, around 50 per cent of the population is under the age of 15.

As if to confirm Vicky's point (that 'practical solutions lie in
listening to men, women, girls and boys on the ground'), the
last letter Alex got raised one practical way of helping to
provide economic support in rural Africa. She'd written to
Glyn Roberts as she'd heard about the work he was doing
through an organisation called Tools For Self Reliance.

Dear Alex,

Do you ever wonder about the friends you made at your village school in Kenya - how they will earn a living?

Millions of youngsters in Africa face the prospect of a lifetime without any regular work. Agriculture needs fewer hands. Modern industry can employ only a tiny minority. So what are these young people to do with their lives? Drift into the cities, and into trouble? As the Prime Minister of neighbouring Tanzania put it, 'Youth unemployment is Africa's time bomb.'

Politicians don't have any answers, not on the scale needed. Nor do business and commerce: their aim is output and profits, not to provide jobs. Even the major aid agencies see employment as a low priority - preferring welfare and disaster work, or investment in projects based on advanced technology.

This is one of today's great contradictions. The rhetoric about aid is pro-environment, and claims that 'the people must be involved in their own development'. Great stuff. But the technology adopted by decision-makers with the big budgets is costly, energy-hungry, even damaging. And, almost invariably, it needs fewer and fewer people to run it.

Is there a way forward? As the big projects fail (and many do) craft work and small enterprises will come into their own. They may not do much for exports, but they will provide goods, services and jobs where the people are. And that's what matters. Hundreds of thousands of such small enterprises exist already, in every town and village.

They won't provide a 'total solution' to the problems of youth unemployment of course, but if any such solution exists, I am sure that this sector will be part of it. That means we are talking hundreds of millions of tools. Where are they to come from?

Tools For Self Reliance, a voluntary agency in Britain, has now collected and refurbished half a million basic hand tools and sewing machines for communities, mostly in Africa. The potential is vast, since some 50 million useful old tools are presently rusting away in the UK. What a waste! I'm sure there are plenty in Northumberland; could your school help collect some?

We also cooperate with village tool-makers, in Tanzania, Zimbabwe, Uganda, Ghana and Sierra Leone. We provide equipment, some transport and training. Recorded tool production for the various schemes has already topped 400,000, which is brilliant.

It won't be easy. I was recently at a South/North conference and tried to get the 'tools' message across in the working groups. One group from the North laughed out loud at the very idea, and I was disappointed that participants from the South kept quiet. Yet later, in the corridors, various Southern delegates came up to me - separately, almost embarrassed - saying, 'I was quite interested by what you had to say. Actually, my organisation does have a problem getting basic tools. How do we contact you?' My response was that, while we would like to help, just tackling individual requests will never solve matters. The only answer is to move 'tools' from being a private problem to a public issue.

I hope your book, *Lifelines*, will help in this process.

Good luck and best wishes,

Glyn Roberts
Founder and Coordinator

Dear Mr Roberts,

Thank you very much for your excellent letter.

Family planning is all very well, but the people are already there and they need jobs. There was a workshop next door to my school at Likoni in Kenya where disabled people who used to be beggars learned how to be carpenters. The trouble was, when they had learned to make beautiful furniture and things, they still didn't have any tools, so I think Tools For Self Reliance is a great idea. My Grandma says she has got dozens of tools in her garage which nobody ever uses, so I have asked her to send them to you by Red Star. The best way to get a lot of tools would be to get children to bring them to school and then send a lorry round collecting them all. I'm sure you could get millions of tools like that.

With best wishes,

Yours sincerely,

Alex Johnston

TIME FOR ACTION!

As Alex pointed out in her letter, there's a terrible book famine in many parts of the world. The situation is so bad in some African countries that 10 school children can end up sharing one textbook.

So why not ask your head teacher to see if *your* school could help out? Old textbooks or sets of reading books that are being replaced are often just chucked out by schools here in the UK. Instead, they could be sent out to a developing country to continue to help children learn and develop. The organisation that can help you coordinate this is Book Aid International, 2 Coldharbour Place, 39-41 Coldharbour Lane, London SE5 9NR, tel: 0171 733 3577.

As part of their Textbooks for Africa Project, they have already sent out over 325,000 to 18 different African countries.

If your head teacher does want to help out with this, contact Book Aid International *first*. And be warned – arranging for the books to get down to London is often as hard as gathering them in.

Chapter 6
SNAPSHOTS OF THE FUTURE

It was hearing about organisations like Book Aid International and Tools For Self Reliance that got Alex off on the last of her quests: to see how many people had an equally positive view of the future and how much can be done to improve things. But it's not easy trying to work out how things that are happening *now* will shape our lives 10 or 20 years into the future.

So Alex thought she would put some well-known people with an interest in the environment to her own 'futures test': what do they think life would be like 15 years off in the year 2010? Here's what she sent them to get their creative juices flowing:

By the year 2010, how will Britain have changed? That's up to you!

My idea of the future in Britain is optimistic, but it depends on *individuals* taking responsibility. If every person in Britain decided it was up to him, or her, to leave their bit of Britain better than they found it, just think what a lovely country Britain could be by the year 2010! It's no good just thinking about it, though, without DOING anything.

Phil Drabble, who did the 'One Man and His Dog' programme on television, is a good example of how one person can leave his bit of Britain better than he found it. He cares much more about his wildlife sanctuary and his heronry than he does about money, and he encourages local school children to learn from his work, so *they* will make sure his little bit of Britain is still thriving in 2010 when they are grown up, even if he is dead by then. Phil Drabble knows he can't take money with him when he dies, and nobody would remember or care how much money he had. But his life's work will survive, and people will remember him when they enjoy it as much as he did.

His is a good example not just for children, but for adults as well. In his opinion, which I agree with, a lot of politicians are 'so totally absorbed in trying to keep their own jobs that they haven't the time to get involved with people or causes which will not get immediate votes'. That means children, and causes which children are interested in, do not concern them, or so they think! It's a good thing there are people like Phil Drabble around, or it would be *impossible* to have an optimistic vision of the future! These are some of the things I think are important.

In 2010 'Birth Trees', planted to mark the birth of a child, will have caught on all over the world. People will have gone a step further by planting 'Marriage Trees', and 'Anniversary Trees', so we end up with Marriage Orchards, and Anniversary Forests.

Villages will have become more self-sufficient, with community centres, a place of worship where everyone can worship in their own way, shops, parks and fields in which trees can be planted. There will be garden space with all the houses, in which most people have greenhouses and grow their own fruit and vegetables from hydroponics systems (see below) which they have been taught how to use at school - since teaching children how to grow their own food has become part of the National Curriculum in Britain.

By 2010, cheap do-it-yourself hydroponic systems have been developed, which anyone can assemble to grow their own fruit and vegetables. These hydroponic systems work by arranging rows of plastic trays (one on top, then another below, then another and another and so on) and growing fruit and vegetables in the trays. The top row is watered with a mixture of water and nutrients, and this mixtures trickles down through the trays so that none is wasted. Surplus water which isn't absorbed by the plants drips into a trough at the bottom and is pumped to the top to be recycled, working by solar battery.

Everyone is much healthier from eating home-grown organic food and those who don't grow their own fruit and vegetables still would not buy anything that was not organically grown and doesn't display an EU Ecolabel, because they know chemical fertilizers, pesticides and weedkillers would damage their health.

Not only has the landscape and the way people live changed, but the people themselves have changed. They know THEY are responsible for the future - not the Government and Big Business.

And because people are relying on themselves and each other much more than they used to, instead of leaving everything to the Government and Big Business, they know each other better and organise to go places together in one car to save petrol. Every community has a 'car-pool' where people who don't need a car all the time can rent one for as long as they want with unlimited mileage. However, most of the time they ride bicycles on safe new cycle-ways.

An International Court for Crimes Against the Planet has been set up. Enemies of the Future don't want any hassles like that, so they too become Friends of the Future!

One of the first to reply was David Puttnam, film producer and tireless defender of the British film industry, with a big interest in many of the communication technologies of the future.

Dear Alex,

At the beginning of the twentieth century about 5 per cent of the world's people lived in cities. At the beginning of the next century, more than 50 per cent will be living in cities.

That poses a huge challenge. Can we plan cities better, making them decent places for people to live? Can we begin to care more effectively for the environment, in cities *and* in the increasingly threatened countryside that surrounds them? Already cities are said to be responsible for more than 90 per cent of global pollution.

All around the world there are people wrestling with these issues in creative ways, working to find the technological solutions we need to be able to improve the quality of life without the unsustainable levels of pollution and the waste of resources that are still the marks of what we regard as 'progress' today.

But the really important changes aren't going to be technological. There will be changes in the way we work together to solve issues and resolve disputes; in other words, how we communicate with each other. Working as I do in the film business, I feel very aware of the enormous changes that are going on in audio-visual and multi-media communications systems. With every day that passes, more people are gaining better access to these media with their vast potential for education, for teaching new skills, for opening up enjoyment and understanding of the arts, for making communication quicker and easier.

Ever since the first cities grew up four or five thousand years ago, they have been the driving force of human society because they bring people together, enabling them to work together and learn from each other. That's why, despite all the drawbacks, they've gone on growing and growing. The new media that are springing up around us at the moment offer a way of carrying some of those benefits forward into the next millennium.

Of course there are all kinds of dangers and difficulties on the way, but I think that is a genuinely exciting prospect, and it fills me with real hope for the future.

Yours sincerely,

David Puttnam

PS I think the book is a wonderful idea!

Dear Mr Puttnam,

Thank you very much for your letter.

It is very encouraging when people say nice things about my project, as you did. Sometimes I wonder if it can really do any good to change anything, but when people like you are so enthusiastic about it, then I think maybe it can.

When Jonathon Porritt (who is editing this book) mentioned this project on the radio, somebody called Roger Rosewell wrote a long article in the *Daily Mail* saying adults shouldn't get children to fight their battles for them. But I was writing letters like this long before anybody suggested doing a book, so it was really unfair to say that. I just hope there are not too many people like Mr Rosewell around, because they could put other children off doing the same thing.

With best wishes.

Yours sincerely,

Alex Johnston

If there *are* a lot of adults around like that, Alex can refer them to Professor Ghillean Prance, Director of the Royal Botanic Gardens at Kew in London. He is one of the world's leading experts on the rainforests and all the wonderful plants and creatures that live in them. For him, the involvement of young people is one of the things that gives him real hope for the future.

Dear Alex,

Congratulations on your visionary project. It is a great encouragement to people like me that the younger generation is doing so much, and your book can only help the cause. I am delighted with your chapter on 'Snapshots of the Future', and especially the fact that you have taken a positive stand about it. We are nearing the limit to be able to take a positive stand on the environment, as world population and hunger increase, but it is still not too late.

I am particularly interested that you caught one of the most important points that is damaging to the environment at present: politicians are indeed only interested in re-election, and do not think long-term. Some of the North American Indians think about the consequences of their actions in terms of the effect it will have on the seventh unborn generation! If we were to adopt that sort of thinking, the world would be a very different place.

I am also glad that you have put an emphasis on public transport, rather than people going to work, as individuals, in a car. I think something else that will happen by 2010 is that vehicles themselves will have changed. I would hope that there is much greater use of electric vehicles, which are not polluting if the electricity is generated from sustainable sources, such as wind generators, photovoltaic cells, etc.

We have just had a bus built to transport disabled people around Kew Gardens. It is powered by electricity and has 500 photovoltaic cells in the roof, so that it gathers most of its energy from daylight rather than the power line. This kind of thing will certainly increase.

Your concept of producing one's vegetables from hydroponic systems is certainly a good possibility, and could be combined with the idea that many people might have fish tanks in which they grew Tilapia or other fish. These could then feed on some of the waste products of the hydroponic systems. I have seen this working in one or two experimental places already, and it produces a *lot* of fish that way.

You rightly talk about planting trees, but we also need to do a lot about preservation of the different types of habitats, so that people will be able to enjoy them, and to observe the plants and birds that we do today, rather than have a greater number of extinctions.

With best wishes.

Yours sincerely,

Professor Ghillean Prance
Director of the Royal Botanic Gardens, Kew

Well, the shopkeeper told me they were Tilapia when I bought them

Dear Professor Prance

Thank you very much for your excellent letter. I loved the idea about people having Tilapia ponds as well as their hydroponics conservatories, and thank you for pointing out the importance of protecting habitats. Adding one extra ingredient to that, what do you think about the idea of designing captive breeding cages and enclosures so that ordinary people can help to preserve endangered insects and small creatures in their hydroponics greenhouses? People could end up being self-sufficient even from their back gardens as well as helping to preserve endangered animals and, of course, plants.

   With best wishes.
   Yours sincerely,

   Alex Johnston

Professor Prance and Alex's next correspondent are the two sides of the same woody coin, one dealing with rainforests and the other with the temperate forests of the northern hemisphere. Dr Oliver Rackham knows as much about the trees, woodlands and forests of the UK as there is to know, and he likes people to get their ecology *right*, even if they can't predict the future!

136

Dear Alex,

I am no good at predicting the future. Did I foresee in 1953 that within two years the rabbits would be dead and there would be little future for chalk grassland? (No.) Did I know in 1960 that within twenty years England would be ruled by the love of money? (No.) Did I predict in 1969 that within twenty-five years a quarter of the arable land in England would no longer be needed? (No, but I could have done.) In an unstable century like ours it is difficult to be forward-thinking.

I was one of the last generation of streetwise children. We wandered around lanes and heaths and ruined buildings. (Bombing in the War had let Nature back into cities.) We took our chances of being run over. We discovered for ourselves how the world worked and what plants and animals were – I was fascinated by toadstools.

Most people today are prisoners of home, school, and playing-field, sitting before the television like convicts in jail, depending on what grown-ups choose to tell them.

What grown-ups choose to tell them is, mostly, what other grown-ups chose to tell *them* when they were students, and may well be untrue! Everyone now believes that a tree is something under human control, a sort of gatepost with leaves on, that comes out of a garden centre and dies when blown down or cut down.

The reality, as I discovered when I was eleven, is that trees are not part of the environment in that way, but mysterious beings with a life of their own. They spring up of their own accord on heaths and inside ruined buildings and in places where there are no more rabbits. They are all different; a pine tree is killed when cut down, but an ash tree isn't.

The present ought to be a Golden Age of ecology, but isn't. The goodwill is often there, but not the knowledge. Our age has a thirst for information but little respect for truth.

137

Political ecology is largely based on a misunderstanding of real ecology.

Ecology is by far the most complex subject that schools teach: it is much more difficult than physics, which is based on a few well-defined natural laws. Teachers do their best, but there is not enough time or opportunity to debunk all errors.

The future of Britain must depend on education. I look into the crystal ball and don't like what I see. To future citizens I would say: be open-minded; use what liberty the motor car has left you; inquire and experiment in your gardens and on holiday; read old books; learn from what people have done in other countries and in past ages; and above all, don't believe the statistics until you are told how they were arrived at!

Best wishes,

Oliver Rackham

Dear Dr Rackham,

Anything which makes me laugh right at the beginning always entices me to read the rest of it, and now I am convinced that you ought to write a book for children because I am sure it would be a great success and children would learn a lot from it.

If 'Lifelines' is successful it will be because of letters like yours. Dad says I'm getting a really good education for the price of some stamps, so he thinks if other parents don't want to do the same thing, by encouraging their children to write letters, then that's their problem! It will be exciting if the idea catches on, though. If millions of children all start writing to you, you had better write a book quickly so you can just write back and say 'buy my book for £6.99'!

Thank you very much for your letter.

With best wishes.

Your sincerely,

Alex Johnston

Oliver Rackham had really thrown down the gauntlet in arguing that 'the future of Britain must depend on education'. So Alex picked that gauntlet up and passed it over promptly to her own headteacher at Hexham Middle School!

As it happens, David Boas had been giving Alex a lot of encouragement with this letter-writing project, but he may not have anticipated being drawn into it himself.

Dear Alex,

An ideal vision of the role of education in 2010!

Before 2010, the nation will not only come to realise that the future health of society is dependent upon a high quality of education being offered to all of its citizens, but be prepared to fund schools at an appropriate level to enable them to deliver what the nation requires.

With adequate funding for education, schools could then begin to demonstrate just how much more could be achieved for individual pupils. Class sizes could be reduced to allow the teacher time to deal with pupils at an individual level; information technology could be installed at sufficient level to enable all pupils to receive individualised teaching programmes. New schools would be built and existing schools modified to enable all pupils to benefit from the rapid expansion of information technology and the vast amount of data available to individuals through the 'information super-highway'.

A better understanding of science and technology will be crucial. Care of the environment will make huge demands upon the education system. The responsibility for the future survival of man on this fragile planet will require pupils to have a fundamental understanding of the interdependency of the various parts of the different ecosystems.

Adults of the future will need to be more flexible than ever before. Our schools will become

---

less involved in passing on knowledge and more involved in teaching pupils how to learn, where to obtain information, how to understand new concepts and how to learn new skills. The curriculum will include education for leisure and recreation. The value of community service will be reinforced and the skills of parenting will be taught to all.

Education becomes the *key* element in creating a more understanding, more caring and more environmentally aware individual. The education system itself will become more adaptable to change, becoming ever more skilful in meeting the rapidly changing needs of pupils.

Yours sincerely,

David Boas
Headteacher, Hexham Middle School

At 90 years of age, Alex's next correspondent is still something special. Max Nicholson helped to set up the World Wide Fund for Nature, and has had a finger in countless green pies both inside and outside of government. He still cares as much about the future today as he did the first day he got involved as a green warrior.

Dear Ms Alexandra Johnston,

Your letter has come in when I am about to leave for meetings in the Mediterranean. But it's kind of you to think of including me in your book. I used to be regarded as a young man in a hurry, but now I should perhaps rather appear as a skeleton at the feast!

I'm going to put to you this awkward question: why are we still making such slow progress in transforming the world to an environmentally friendly system? I put it to you that, despite all that we have learnt about ecology and conservation, we are still clinging too much to a well-meaning missionary approach, and are failing to recognise that the only proven way of injecting revolutionary principles into society is by creating a powerful, well-trained profession. Examples are the law, which has taught us the hard way to accept the rule of law as an essential; or science, which has stopped us pursuing emotive lines of thought and taught us how to recognise facts; or engineering, which has converted us to the uses of technology.

How are we going to learn to apply this proven method to the environment, rather than preaching to those who don't want to know?

Science, education, decision-makers and the media desperately need reliable information to transform our world into an efficient, environmentally-friendly habitat for ourselves as well as nature. We should THINK BIG and MOVE FAST!

To do this we need to be less kind and tolerant to those who are selfishly and stupidly ruining the planet for us all. We should be giving more support to such bodies as Friends of the Earth and Greenpeace, and encourage them to issue a public Black List of policies and practices which amount to grave environmental misconduct. Those on the Black List should be publicly advised what they have to do to get off it, and should be given no rest until they comply!

Perhaps our fault as environmentalists has been that we are just too nice for the world we have to live in?

With best wishes, in haste.

Yours,

Max Nicholson

Dear Mr Nicholson,

Thank you very much for your letter. I think most people of ninety are asleep at 5 o'clock in the morning and not many of them would be going to meetings in the Mediterranean so you must be very fit for your age!

   With best wishes,

                    Alex Johnston

Max Nicholson and Bill Oddie (together with a frighteningly large number of correspondents in this chapter) would certainly agree on the limitations of modern politicians.

Dear Alex,
Many thanks for your letter. I've no idea why I didn't receive it back in July - but I didn't! Maybe the Government interrupted it because it contained so much sense.

   I agree with every word you say - so I haven't actually got that much to add.

   But what I would say is this: please, please make sure you go into politics! As you are obviously aware, most of the wicked ways of the world are dictated by ambitious, greedy and corrupt politicians. There's rather a lot of them in this Government at the moment, I reckon. It is absolutely essential that the right people get into power. So please become one of those people - for all our sakes.

   Love and best wishes,

                    Bill Oddie

Looking forward to a better future often involves looking back to things lost in the past. Kathleen Raine is one of the country's leading contemporary poets and a renowned expert on the works of that great visionary poet, William Blake. Like Alex, she too acquired a lot of her early inspiration from the rolling Northumberland countryside.

Dear Alexandra Johnston,

You show great enterprise in asking us what we would *like* the future of the land of Britain to be. I too had a country childhood in Northumberland long ago, so that country world is very dear to me. But technology has its own momentum, and it is unlikely that the horse will return to plough the land or skilled hedgers and ditchers to tend the roadsides.

However, a return to organic agriculture might be brought about. *I* would like to see an end to pesticides and artificial fertilizers which pollute and poison rivers and water supplies. I would like to see an end to destroying old pasture with its rich flora. I would like to see the end of the rearing of cattle and pigs in those narrow stalls. I would like to see the end of hedge-cutting by machines which level hedges to the height convenient to the machine, rather than the hedges I remember which were high and thick enough to support a population of birds and small animals. I'm afraid my future seems to be looking back rather a lot!

Equally unlikely is the restoration of rural communities, with people living on the land who love it and understand land and animals. Something might be done by 'New Age' communities of committed people who reject – as I do – the commercial values prevailing in our present society.

At the heart of it all is the absence in this country of any spiritual vision or spiritual wisdom. This too is possible, and without it, I see little hope. That's one reason why I would like to see Prince Charles as King of this country, as almost the one man in public life who understands such things.

However, one thing is certain: the future is never what is predicted by the experts! Radical changes sometimes come about not gradually but suddenly, almost overnight. And I believe only in the unexpected.

With all good wishes,

Kathleen Raine

Dear Mrs Raine,

Thank you very much for your excellent letter, which arrived in the post this morning. When I read it out aloud to Mum and Dad, Mum kept saying 'but this is MY vision, this echoes EVERYTHING I want to see!'

It will be very interesting to see how all the visions compare with each other. I had a lovely one yesterday from Max Nicholson who is ninety, and he was in a hurry to go to a meeting in the Mediterranean, so he typed it up at 5 o'clock in the morning! He started by saying he used to be seen as a young man in a hurry, but now he feels more like a skeleton at the feast! It sounded to me as if nothing has changed with him at all, except that how he is an *old* man in a hurry!

With best wishes.

Yours sincerely,

Alex Johnston

PS Dad was very pleased to see that you have an ancient typewriter like his. He thinks computers are a substitute for thinking about things, so he refused to get one. He even thinks his typewriter has a soul! He wants to start an Ancient Typewriter Association as a rebellion against computers. But I doubt if many people would agree with him - including me! He has had two offers of a free computer and turned them both down. I still haven't forgiven him!

I suspect Alex's Dad would recruit more supporters to his Association than Alex imagines! It is possible that people in the future may think rather differently about new technologies, questioning the assumption that they automatically improve things or make things easier for us.

That's certainly the case for Jeremy Paxman, the intrepid and much feared BBC interviewer and more recently host of University Challenge.

Dear Alex,

Thank you for your letter about your book.

2010 is a very precise date to choose. If, instead of looking forward, you look back 15 years, how life has changed! Faxes, home computers, video recorders, microwaves, CDs, were all either uninvented or uncommon. It therefore seems to me inevitable that the onward march of technology will provide a whole raft of consumer gizmos with which those who can afford them will make life easier. Machines will become more reliable with every passing year, which I suppose is another good thing.

But if you ask me whether this technological process makes us any happier, I'd have to answer 'probably not'. The whole trend of technology is towards a fragmented community, with fewer and fewer shared experiences. I think this is bound to make for a much more disjointed society.

I'm sorry if this sounds gloomy. Scientific progress *could* offer so much, but I'm not sure it will.

Yours sincerely,

Jeremy Paxman

Dear Mr Paxman,

Thank you very much for your excellent letter.

Your letter reminded me of one from Dr Oliver Rackham, which started 'I am not very good at predicting the future. I didn't predict . . . ' and then a long list of all the things he didn't predict! I had the same problem as well. It's interesting what you say about 'technological progress'. If you saw the number of people who have answered my 'Snapshots' essay saying I haven't given them time to think, maybe technology has already stopped people from being able to think! Some of the best letters I have received were obviously written in about *five minutes*, so there's still some hope for the future.

Africans in Kenya, where we used to live, do seem to be happier than people in England to judge by the way they laugh at everything, and they haven't got much technology or anything else!

With best wishes.

Yours sincerely,

Alex Johnston

It's the one drawback with the low energy low life bulb

Nicholas Albery, Director of an organisation called the Institute for Social Inventions, would be the first to appreciate the significance of that last point. Having more money is *not* the same thing as being happier.

However, his vision got both Alex and her Dad thinking very seriously indeed about what the future has in store for them.

Dear Alexandra Johnston,

Thank you for your letter. I think the year 2010 could be OK, but that it will get worse before it gets better. Here are some of my thoughts about the future - I've concentrated on what it might be like up there in Northumberland!

Britain as such no longer exists. This is all to the good. But it has taken a terrible tragedy to bring it about.

In August 2006 an unidentified Islamic fundamentalist group failed in its attempt to blackmail the French government. On August 21st, the group carried out its threat and exploded a number of nuclear devices smuggled into Paris, and destroyed most of the city. Similar blackmail was directed against other Western cities, and our national societies fell apart. Local areas vetted newcomers and strangers very carefully to ensure that they represented no security danger. Travel and immigration became very restricted.

As a result, the world in 2010 is now entirely fragmented politically, like a ship with watertight compartments. The British Isles are simply a loose commonwealth of independent republics. The old county of Northumberland, for instance, is now The Free and Independent Republic of Northumberland. It has its own (entirely electronic) currency, stamps, national theatre, prime minister, parliament, armed forces etc. Villages and parishes within towns very much run their own affairs by referenda. The local

---

policeman goes round each household once a
fortnight to ask if residents have seen anything
suspicious in their area.

Each village imposes a labour tax on its
residents - they must each work two hours a week
for the neighbourhood on anything from street
cleaning to care for the elderly. Or, if unable to
do so because of pressure of work elsewhere, they
pay a labour tax so that the neighbourhood can
employ someone else who is less busy.

Each neighbourhood has its own 'caretaker'.
The quality of life in each neighbourhood very
much depends on the quality of its caretaker, as
this person has many roles - from coordinating
neighbourhood watch to work allocation.

Population figures continue to go down;
the taxation system rewards those with fewest
children. It's all part of a campaign to make
Northumberland as self-sufficient in food and
manufactures as possible.

Despite the human tragedies that have
afflicted the West so recently, people in
Northumberland are relatively happy nowadays. The
churches and chapels have full congregations,
mainly of teenagers. Northumberland has a
reputation among the ten thousand nations for the
quality of its mystics.

How does that strike you?

With best wishes,

Nicholas Albery

For many people, that kind of vision of the future is not
so much a utopia as an anti-utopia! Alex didn't know
whether to add it to the pile of 'optimists' replies' or
'pessimists' replies'. She had no such difficulty with the next
letter from Chris Packham, TV presenter and star of the
'Really Wild Show'.

Dear Alexandra,

Thank you for your letter kindly inviting my vision of the future. I would like to be as optimistic as you are about the outlook for our country, but I'm afraid that I see a rather uncomfortable, over-crowded and aggressive Britain by the year 2010.

I have no doubt that all of those who work so hard now to conserve species or areas of land will continue to do so. So I'm sure that there will be some small and beautiful patches of Britain left. But I fear that these will be lost in a huge ugly sprawl of roads and new developments.

I see Britain's problem as the same problem which confronts the entire planet: that we are becoming increasingly overcrowded. We are also victims of insane political greed, road building madness and ecological insensitivity. But if there were fewer of us, each of these other factors wouldn't be so serious. Until the population in Britain, and worldwide, begins to fall significantly, the outlook for the future in terms of our own comfort and survival becomes increasingly bleak.

With such a grim outlook, you could ask why do I bother, or why do we all bother to recycle, conserve, and improve our environment? I don't think that pessimism is any excuse for a slovenly mental or spiritual attitude. To remain true to ourselves, we must all contribute everything we can to attain the highest goals. If only more people in business and government shared this motivation – as *you* obviously do.

Yours sincerely,
With all best wishes,

Chris Packham

Spike Milligan out-gloomed even that gloomy vision!

Dear Alexandra,

In future, due to overpopulation, the world will be crowded to bursting point. While animals will have been exterminated by human pressure, the countryside will be one mass of motorways and millions of cars sending out fumes into the atmosphere.

That is my opinion of the future; sorry it's so glum, but I am facing up to the truth. Even as I speak, millions are being born.

Sincerely,
Spike Milligan

Alex was not too happy about leaving her patient readers 'on a bit of a down'. So at the very last moment she stuck one last letter in the post – to her Editor!

Dear Jonathon,

As the top of my hit list sorry, a top environmentalist! I am sure you have lots of ideas of how
you would like Britain to be by the year 2010.
There must be lots of people who would be interested in your views on how things are likely to
turn out, especially ME!

Just a few guidelines: I do NOT want a
miserable grey world with bombs dropping all over
it, nor do I want the world covered in advertising
posters for political parties, charities for
con-men, cigarettes and booze and other expensive
rubbish that I don't want or need. In your crystal
ball, I do not wish you to see cardboard boxes
full of starving people all the way to the
horizon, without a tree or a blade of grass or a
little critter anywhere in sight. I DO want a
world where EVERYBODY'S opinions will be respected
whether they are black or white or Muslims or
Christians, etc.

When I was at the Ferry School in Kenya, we
used to sing a song which I can still remember
some of the words of because it was the only song
we sang in English. The song went like this: 'A
child is black, a child is white, together we
learn to read and write, read and write, a-rum-
dum-dum. And now a child can understand, this is
the law of all the land, all the land, a-rum-dum-
dum'. I suppose 'the law of all the land' in the
song is that we're all the same, so that must be
YOUR vision of the future as well.

I hope that is clearly understood!

And just to cause you the maximum amount of
pain and anguish, the deadline for your vision is
tomorrow!

With kind regards,

Alex

Dear Alex,

I am really not sure that this is such a good
idea! The last time I tried to explain my
vision of the future (for the BBC *Wildlife
Magazine*) I had all sorts of well-known
people (including Libby Purves in a leader in
The Times) leaping on me from a great height
saying that I was a menace to society with my
boring, homespun green dreams!

But I shall not be deterred! My vision
of the future is actually very simple, as
life itself will need to become much simpler
if we are to get through the looming
ecological crisis.

By the year 2010 I too see people
living in smaller communities (or in much
better defined 'urban villages' if they live
in cities), making and selling more of the
things they need locally, particularly food.
Good, healthy organic food!

Because there won't be so many full
time jobs to go round, more people will have
a mix of different kinds of work, some of it
paid, some not, some at home, some at a
variety of different workplaces. New
computer and communication technologies
will have revolutionised the way we work.
Having a job will not be the be-all-and-end-
all of life; being happy and more fulfilled
will.

(I realise that sounds a bit naff, but
one of the reasons society is falling apart
with so many desperately unhappy people is
because everything is still geared to getting
those people into full time jobs for 40 or 50
years of their life when it is blindingly
obvious that such jobs are never going to be
there again.)

As far as the environment itself is concerned, people will be able to breathe deeply again - there will be far fewer cars, far better public transport, and people in towns and cities will be walking or cycling much more. Cigarettes will cost so much that only a hard core of people with money (and their lungs) to burn will smoke themselves into an early grave. We will all be a lot fitter and healthier, which means paying far less to keep the National Health Service running.

Our rivers will be restored to their former quality, and water from the tap will not only be safe (which for the vast majority of people in this country it already is), but will taste good. That probably doesn't mean much to you living up there in rural Northumberland, but for us townies, that would be like drinking nectar!

Need I add anything on education? Not when you've got teachers like yours!

As to the rest of the world, it's harder to be optimistic. Popular pressures are still so great, and many still think our model of 'progress' is the only one that works. Despite all the evidence that it really isn't working anymore.

We have also got a lot to learn from the so-called Third World. I suspect in the future we too will once again be doing more things together with friends and family, instead of sitting there plugged into the television on our own, or 'grazing' our food alone instead of eating together. It's not just BT and the water companies that have been privatised: we do more and more in the privacy of our own living rooms and of our brains. 'Virtual reality' is already with us - and it stinks.

So what I want to say above all is that life will be much more fun! We will have more time to read or garden or surf the Internet. We will have more fun celebrating the beauty of the Earth, the creativity of the human spirit, and the gift of life itself.

If I am still alive, I'll be 60 in 2010. If this book works, and you lot do your stuff by bombarding my lot (today's so-called 'decision-makers') with so many letters that they feel they are drowning in the passion, anger and concern of young people, then I should be able to retire happily to learn how to bake bread (something I've been trying to get round to for the last 20 years) and hoe my organic row, and plant trees.

Which means I am putting the ball firmly back into your court - this book is just the start. I am counting on you!

Best wishes,

Jonathon

TIME FOR ACTION!

What about doing a vision of your own for the year 2010?

You could then send it off to Alex (care of her publishers) or better still to your own Member of Parliament.

And while you're at it, why not challenge him or her to come up with a vision of their own. Politicians have come in for a lot of stick in Lifelines (not least from Alex herself!) but they're not *all* that bad. Some care as much about the future and the well-being of the planet Earth and its people as any of those whose voice has been heard in these pages. So why not see if *your* MP is one of those?

Postscript by Alex

(Can't let Jonathon Porritt have the last word!)

Dear Reader,

If you want to make changes for a better future, how do YOU go about it? Do you march through the streets, your protest banner held high? Or join an environmental organisation, and buy things from all their trading catalogues? Or pester your parents and teachers?

If these are your ways of voicing your opinion, then carry on. They definitely make a difference. But do enough people listen, I mean REALLY listen? Do people who CAN make rapid changes think, 'Hey - those protesters have got a point!' or do they just dismiss your opinions? Do the looters of the planet wonder, 'am I in the wrong?'

Letter-writing is like fishing. You KNOW when you've got a result!

Of course, if you are rude and 'loud' and fixed
⸻ ⸻ions, then your fish won't bite. Best
⸻ ⸻ able! There's nothing
⸻ DY can get results - but
⸻ ything you can get your
⸻ ich you intend to do

⸻ really love to hear
⸻ ght about any of the
⸻ book is not the same
⸻ don't know who you
⸻ or what your interests
⸻ ear from you.
⸻ ng something of your
⸻ or have ideas about
things you ⸻
It's probably best ⸻ o write to me at the publishers, Red Fox.

Alex Johnston
c/o Red Fox
Random House Children's Books
20 Vauxhall Bridge Road
London SW1V 2SA

Best wishes,
Alex Johnston

Resources and Addresses

Animal Aid
(The Old Chapel, Bradford Street, Tonbridge, Kent TN9 1AW, tel 01732 364546)
Animal Aid campaigns on a wide range of animal welfare issues, including animal experimentation, factory farming and circuses. It believes in peaceful, strictly non-violent protest, and has stood out against the use of violence in the animal rights movement. They have some excellent ideas for schools-based campaigning, and have established a network of local youth groups serviced with a regular newsletter called *Youth Rage*.

British Trust for Conservation Volunteers (BTCV)
(36 St Mary's Street, Wallingford, Oxfordshire OX10 0EU, tel 01491 839766)
BTCV is the best known of the organisations that get people out there actually *doing* it: restoring hedgerows, planting trees, establishing footpaths and so on. They have a schools membership service, and are very keen to engage the interest of as many young people as possible.

British Union for the Abolition of Vivisection (BUAV)
(16a Crane Grove, London N7 8LB, tel 0171 700 4888)
Relying on detailed research and undercover investigations, the BUAV campaigns for an end to animal experiments. Recent campaigns have focused on cosmetic testing, the trade in wild-caught primates (monkeys) for research and genetic engineering. The BUAV's 'Approved Product Guide' lists 200 companies which sell 'cruelty-free' cosmetics and toiletries. They also have a schools project pack, including an 18 page colour booklet 'Animal Experiments: A Reference Guide for Schools', which is available free to enquirers.

City Farms
(National Federation of City Farms, 93 Whitby Road, Brislington, Bristol BS4 3QF, tel 01179 719109)
There are more than 60 city farms around the country (most of

them signed up as organisations of the National Federation of City Farms), attracting more than 2.5 million visits a year. They are very different from zoos or wildlife parks, encouraging active participation from visitors and taking on a lot of training activities. Each city farm offers slightly different facilities.

Friends of the Earth
(26-28 Underwood Street, London N1 7JQ, tel 0171 490 1555)
Friends of the Earth campaigns on a wider range of issues than any other organisation in the UK. It has excellent information leaflets and other publications for young people, and although it no longer has a special youth organisation, membership for anyone under the age of 18 is half the usual price. Its newsletter *Earth Matters* is a particularly good read, with its own children's section.

Greenpeace
(Canonbury Villas, London N1 2PM, tel 0171 354 5100)
Greenpeace is probably the best known campaigning organisation in the world, particularly on marine and nuclear issues. It has some very useful fact sheets, but does not organise any activities specifically for young people. Greenpeace local groups are very big on fundraising.

Learning Through Landscapes
(Third Floor, Southside Offices, The Law Courts, Winchester, Hants SO23 9DL, tel 01962 846258)
Learning Through Landscapes is the one charity in the UK working to make school grounds (especially playgrounds) both user-friendly and environment-friendly. If you want to stir your teachers into action to convert your concrete wasteland into a green oasis, LTL can show you how it's done and how to set about it without further delay.

The National Trust
(33 Sheep Street, Cirencester, Gloucestershire GL7 1QW, tel 01285 651818)
The National Trust is the biggest conservation charity in the UK, looking after both historic houses and particularly special areas of countryside – including 520 miles of coastline. It has a Junior

Member category with its own Newsletter, and has recently been developing a 'Guardianship' scheme which allows schools to become directly involved in any local National Trust property.

The Pedestrians' Association
(126 Aldersgate Street, London EC1A 4JQ, tel 0171 490 0750)
The Pedestrians' Association doesn't actually arrange any special activities for young people, but they have a very hard-hitting action pack designed to make local councillors and business people think again about the importance of walking – and of making our towns and cities safe for pedestrians of all ages.

The Ramblers' Association
(1–5 Wandsworth Road, London SW8 2SX, tel 0171 582 6878)
This is a dynamic and fast-growing organisation which campaigns to protect footpaths and improve access to the countryside. As well as 370 local groups, which organise regular walks and other activities, they have had more and more young members taking part in these activities. The annual 'Family Rambling Day' is a great success.

Royal Society for the Prevention of Cruelty to Animals
(Causeway, Horsham, Sussex RH12 1HG, tel 01403 264181)
The RSPCA (which campaigns for the prevention of all forms of cruelty to animals) has an Animal Action Club for anyone under 17, which will provide you with a host of useful ideas and information materials, including a magazine for young people called *Animal World*. It also organises several interesting projects, competitions and fundraising events.

Royal Society for the Protection of Birds
(The Lodge, Sandy, Beds SG12 2DL, tel 01767 680551)
The RSPB is one of the biggest environmental organisations in the UK – concentrating mostly on birds, but dealing with many other countryside and conservation questions as well. The Young Ornithologists Club is for the under 16s (there are already 120,000 of them and 250 YOC groups), and is one of the best run organisations for young people you will find. Schools can also become members and take part in various RSPB activities.

Tools for Self-Reliance (see page 124)
(Netley Marsh, Southampton SO40 7GY, tel 01703 869697)
Tools for Self-Reliance was set up in 1979 by a group of volunteers who had just returned from working in Africa. They had seen at first hand the shortage of simple hand tools in many developing countries. There are now around 60 TFSR groups around the country, and in 1994 more than half a million tools were sent overseas.

The Wildlife Trusts
(The Green, Witham Park, Waterside South, Lincoln LN5 7JR,
tel 01522 544400)
There are lots of Wildlife Trusts around the country, organised on a county basis. Wildlife WATCH is their 'action club for young environmentalists', with local groups organising a wide range of activities and projects, including Frog WATCH, Owl WATCH and even Rock WATCH! The UK subscription to Wildlife WATCH includes three issues of the magazine, *WATCHWORD*, and a local newsletter.

Women's Environmental Network
(Aberdeen Studios, 22 Highbury Grove, London N5 2EA,
tel 0171 354 8823)
WEN is the only environmental group in the UK which specifically represents women's interests. It doesn't have a separate youth organisation, but what it does have is some excellent information leaflets about the kind of issues other organisations tend to avoid, like packaging, sanitary protection products, false labelling claims and so on. It also does a lot of work in schools, and provides speakers wherever possible.

World Wide Fund for Nature
(Panda House, Weyside Park, Godalming, Surrey GU7 1XR,
tel 01483 426444)
WWF campaigns all around the world for the protection of threatened species and habitats. *Go Wild!* is no longer a membership club, but still provides free information for young people, and is very keen to get even more of them involved in fundraising at the local level.

Index of Contributors